Cold
Crematorium

Cold
Crematorium

REPORTING FROM THE LAND OF AUSCHWITZ

József Debreczeni

Translated from the Hungarian by
Paul Olchváry

Foreword by
Jonathan Freedland

ST. MARTIN'S PRESS
NEW YORK

First published in the United States by St. Martin's Press, an imprint of St. Martin's Publishing Group

www.stmartins.com

Design by Meryl Sussman Levavi

Map by Laura Hartman Maestro, original schematic courtesy of the United States Holocaust Memorial Museum

Library of Congress Cataloging-in-Publication Data

Names: Debreczeni, József, 1905–1978, author. | Olchváry, Paul, translator.
Title: Cold crematorium : reporting from the land of Auschwitz / József
    Debreczeni ; translated from the Hungarian by Paul Olchváry.
Other titles: Hideg krematórium. English
Description: First U.S. edition. | New York : St. Martin's Press, 2023.
Identifiers: LCCN 2023027451 | ISBN 9781250290533 (hardcover) |
    ISBN 9781250290540 (ebook)
Subjects: LCSH: Debreczeni, József, 1905–1978. | Auschwitz
    (Concentration camp)—Biography. | Holocaust, Jewish (1939–1945)—
    Serbia—Personal narratives. | World War, 1939–1945—Prisoners and
    prisons, German. | Jews, Hungarian—Serbia—Vojvodina—Biography. |
    Vojvodina (Serbia)—Biography.
Classification: LCC DS135.H93 D43 2024 | DDC 940.5318092 [B]—
    dc23/eng/20230613
LC record available at https://lccn.loc.gov/2023027451

Originally published as HIDEG KREMATÓRIUM in 1950 by Testvériség-Egység Könyvk, Novi Sad, Serbia; republished in 1975 and 2015 by Forum Könyvkiadó, Novi Sad, Serbia.

First U.S. edition: 2023

10 9 8 7 6 5 4 3 2 1

To the memory of my loved ones

*József Debreczeni with his parents and his wife. Only József would survive Auschwitz;
the rest were murdered upon their arrival at the camp.*

József Debreczeni at his desk

What is any damn thing worth
While weeds run riot over earth
And poisons fail to crush it?

What's winter or the summer for
When my mother's murderer
Still lives and thrives a fascist?

He may yet live or he may not
He may yet breathe and stuff his gut
The priest might have absolved him

He won't be haunted, live in fear,
A song might nestle in his ear
And sunlight may well bronze him.

Heroes and prophets pass him by
Poetry, science, leave him dry:
Are there blessings set and waiting?

Mothers have been born in vain
Into the gas chambers they came
Their children at breast, suckling

It leaves him laughing as they go
The gas once more begins to flow
Time grinds out hell's new kingdom

Dagger and atom now align
More dreadful still when they combine,
Pick up where they began

What is man expecting now?
What point in beating breast or brow?
While showers spew out murder?

All his guilt is in the past.
He finds a new uniform at last,
And poses where he killed her.

                    Translated by George Szirtes

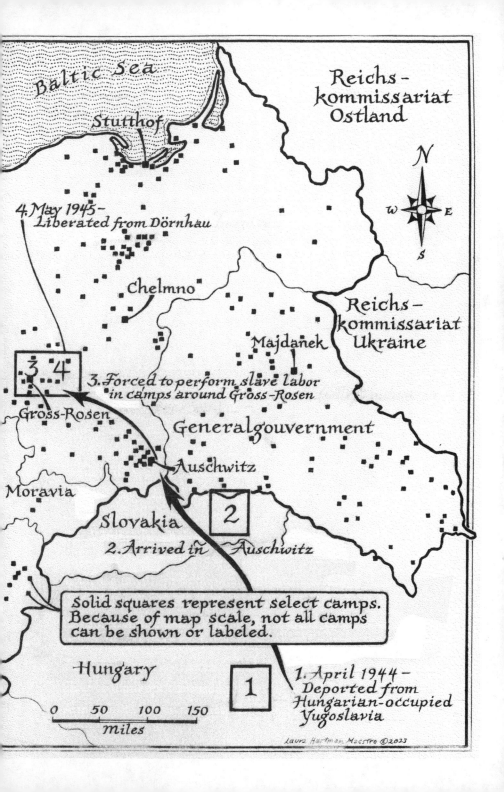

Foreword

The laws of physics dictate that the farther away an object is, the smaller it appears. But the Holocaust does not obey that rule. The Nazi attempt to eliminate the Jewish people is eight decades away, and yet it only seems to loom larger, the scale of the horror more striking and more shocking as it grows more distant. What's more, instead of becoming blurrier as it recedes from view, we now see it in sharper detail. That is thanks in no small part to the emergence—or exhumation—of remarkable accounts like this one by József Debreczeni.

In a way, it makes a perverse sense that the Holocaust should defy what we think of as the laws of nature. For those were devised for Planet Earth, while the Holocaust seemed to take place in a different realm altogether. One survivor famously spoke of Planet Auschwitz, a place where the usual laws of moral gravity did not apply, where evil was good, black was white, and night was day. Debreczeni nods in that same direction toward the close of this book. After liberation, he meets people from "the outside world . . . They are the Martians of the universe beyond the barbed wire."

Debreczeni's testimony itself has reached us like a message from a distant planet, his words arriving decades after he set

them down. First published in 1950, in the relative freedom of
Tito's Yugoslavia, where the Budapest-born Debreczeni lived
after the war, they were lost for a while in the static of the cold
war: the author's praise for his Red Army liberators deemed too
much for the anti-communist stomachs of the West, while his
insistence that it was Jews, rather than the more nebulous category
of "victims of fascism," who had been singled out for annihilation
proved unpalatable to the Stalinists of the East. In a Yugoslavia
non-aligned between the two power blocs, Debreczeni found an
audience initially receptive to his story—which was written in
Hungarian, one of the country's official minority languages, and
produced by a state-owned publisher. But that did not last long.
By the 1960s and 1970s, Yugoslavia had become a colder house
for Jews.

Still, now we have the book—and it was worth the wait. The
library of Holocaust testimony is vast and expanding; neverthe-
less, Debreczeni delivers something of singular value. It's not only
that his are the recollections of a fully conscious adult—when
so many accounts are, necessarily, confined to the memories
of a child—but that he writes as a professional, highly skilled
observer. He is a good noticer, with a journalist's eye for the
telling, human detail. Crammed with other Jews from the Bačka
region of Serbia into the goods train that will take them to Auschwitz, he sees Mr. Mandel, an old man, a friend of his father's, a
carpenter, now deprived of the cigarettes that had been his staple:
"For sixty years he'd smoked fifty a day. Not a man alive had
ever seen Mr. Mandel without a smoldering cigarette . . . On the
train his right hand sometimes moved mechanically, as if holding a cigarette. Between his index and middle fingers Mr. Mandel

raised the imagined cigarette to wilted lips. Like a child pretending to smoke, he even pursed his lips to puff."

Good as he is at seeing the trees, Debreczeni never loses sight of the larger forest. He grasps that he is now a witness to the darkest possibilities of human nature, that he is seeing the desperate depths to which people will sink when they are deprived of the essentials for physical survival, none more basic than food. He is witness, survivor, victim, and also analyst, offering ruminations on some of the enduring questions raised by the Holocaust, among them the puzzle of how arguably the most cultured nation in Europe could have led the continent's descent into the most brutal savagery:

This is a singular people. A bunch of inner contradictions, a bunch of dumbfounding extremes, a singular people that has given the world not only [Nobel Prize winner] Robert Koch but also Ilse Koch, the Witch of Buchenwald, the most perverse woman serial killer of all time, not only [the astronomer] Kepler, but also Himmler . . . Both those obsessed with understanding and the gravediggers of civilization.

The result is a book that, across a mere two-hundred-odd pages, shines a light into corners of the Shoah we may not have seen. Of course, some observations will be familiar enough, though they are put here starkly—starting with the cruelty that became routine on that bleak planet. We see one tormentor, supposedly a medic, "jump up and down on a patient's chest like a rubber ball, stomping on him with bloodshot eyes until he was worn out. The victim's crime: he'd tried conniving his way to a second helping of soup." Debreczeni also reminds us that the victims did not know their imminent fate—a fact crucial to understanding how the Final Solution was possible—and that so many others most certainly did. Describing his journey to the death camp, the author writes: "None of us ... knew about Auschwitz. But the bayonet-adorned Hungarian policemen the Germans had positioned every fifty meters along the road, they knew." That same sentence carries a reminder that, while the eradication of the Jews may have been a project initiated by Berlin, it relied on accomplices recruited across occupied Europe, many only too eager to join the mission of extermination. Active collaboration was aided by the willful blindness of those who, despite living at or near the scene of the crime, would later claim to have seen nothing. At one point, Debreczeni describes a passenger train that passes alongside wagons packed with deportees—"No one looked twice at us"—and wonders, "had death trains become an everyday sight by now?"

Much of what is laid bare in *Cold Crematorium* will come as a shock even to those who consider themselves broadly familiar with the facts of the Holocaust. For what does the average twenty-first-century citizen know of Auschwitz? Perhaps that Jews arrived in cattle cars and were led into what they thought were showers, where they were gassed to death, their bodies turned to ash in ovens. This account, like others published in recent years, shows how incomplete that picture is.

For one thing, Debreczeni was only briefly in the camp we think of as Auschwitz. Instead, he was held in three separate subcamps within a vast network that stretched across the region: those three were satellites of Gross-Rosen, which itself was initially a subcamp of Sachsenhausen. Debreczeni referred to this broader archipelago of horror as "The Land of Auschwitz." Here, those Jews who had survived the initial selection—sent not to the left, to be gassed, but to the right, so that they might be worked to death—were used as slaves, fed almost nothing, kept in conditions that would shame livestock, and subjected to permanent, arbitrary violence. They were tasked with the most back-breaking work: it might be mining or the excavation and construction of subterranean tunneling—apparently to create an underground refuge for German forces facing defeat and retreat.

Their daily tormentors were not, as many readers might imagine, only Nazi Germans or even the Nazis' local collaborators wearing the gray-green uniforms of the SS. In this book, the Germans are mostly out of view and off stage: they are the ultimate authority, the masters of the camp, but their will is done by others. Those others are the kapos, the prisoners picked—often entirely at random—to serve as the Nazis' enforcers, armed both with truncheons and, deployed no less cruelly, the power to distribute the camp's meager resources—the most precious of which is food.

These are the men whom the author and, thanks to the precision of his pen, his reader come to despise. When all around them are starving, each prisoner allocated no more than the exact, scientifically calculated minimum number of calories required for a human being to survive—"just enough nutrients, absolutely necessary to maintain life. To maintain it, not to protect it. The latter isn't important at all"—those kapos charged with handing out bread or ladling out soup show their fellow inmates a callousness that will disturb anyone who imagined solidarity among slaves. They skim off a bit of each portion for themselves and their chums, using their gains for trade. Debreczeni discovers that, even as he and others were subsisting on slivers of bread, margarine, and soup too thin to merit the name, a matter of yards away, in his locked quarters, one of these super-kapos had amassed "boxes upon boxes of cheese and mountains of bread." Sometimes their brutality is more direct. That sadist who made a sport of jumping up and down on the bellies and chests of frail, famished men too weak to resist: he was not an SS officer but a fellow prisoner.

To be clear, Debreczeni knows who the true villains are. He knows that when a senior kapo administers fifty lashes of the whip to a luckless inmate, he does so with vigor because standing over him is the SS sergeant who ordered the flogging—and "if the camp god suspects shenanigans it often happens that the blows continue on the head of the one meting out the sentence."

He understands the psychological trick that is being played on him and the rest of the *häftlinge*, or prisoners, directing their loathing away from the lords of the Auschwitz universe and toward those who, to secure their own survival, have become the masters' henchmen. It is a "diabolically imaginative Nazi system" that understands and exploits human nature, including that "old supposition—proven true on countless occasions—that the best slave driver is a slave accorded a privileged position." The Nazis can maintain total control over three thousand men with just two hundred men of their own in part because they have guns, but also because they have deployed the timeless stratagem of the conqueror: divide and rule.

Debreczeni describes all this as both guinea pig in and observer of a vicious social experiment. He is struck not only by the speed with which a new pecking order takes shape, how fast a fresh kapo kingpin is surrounded by courtiers, but also by the pattern that prevails among the Jewish members of the enforcer class: "Such towering figures of the Auschwitz hierarchy were recruited from among those who, back home, had stood on the bottom rungs of Jewish society. Those who'd made nothing of themselves—schnorrers, nebbishes, schlemiels, freeloaders, rogues, swindlers, idlers, slackers—all blossomed in this swamp."

The author notices too a crucial fact that has eluded many—though not all—chroniclers of the Holocaust. Perhaps because murder is a graver crime than larceny, the economic function of Auschwitz is too often overlooked. But Debreczeni sees it. He understands that the worldly goods of those shipped to Auschwitz in freight trains, whether they be clothes, shoes, human hair, or gold teeth, were dispatched to Germany for sale or use—that the Jews were a resource to be exploited to the last ounce, their possessions, their labor, and their bodies a means for the Reich either to make or save money.

The details he provides on this are stark. Debreczeni names names, spelling out precisely which German corporations maintained an on-the-ground presence, using Jewish slaves as their workforce. In the subcamp of Eule, for example, he reports, "The work is carried out by three companies. The Waldenburg branch of Georg Urban Civil and Structural Engineering AG leases most of the digging work; Kemna AG drills tunnels; and Baugesellschaft builds the structures in what is planned to be a sprawling city of barracks."

These companies were so embedded in the death camp, so integrated in its operations, that prisoners would have company names on their striped uniforms. Officials of these companies acted as overseers and slavemasters, cheerfully reporting to the SS those Jewish inmates they deemed to be slacking—thereby sentencing them to death. A reporter to his fingertips, Debreczeni supplies the key facts: "For my labor the company pays

Hitler's state two marks a day to cover my 'board' and my 'apparel,' and I harbor no illusions that I won't have to earn this sum with blood."

The SS architects of the Land of Auschwitz always intended it to be an economic hub, a throbbing industrial center, but there is another, more intimate economy Debreczeni describes. Once more, as if from the pages of a study in anthropology, he sketches the illicit trade among the prisoners themselves—in crumbs, morsels, and discarded cigarette ends, the currency of those who have nothing.

"It's become widespread practice for even the living to sell the treasures lurking in their oral cavities. A whole army of häftlinge has come to specialize in extracting gold for modest compensation from the mouths of those who volunteer. It's mainly the kitchen workers who buy such gold, in exchange for soup. One gold crown yields special soup every day for a week. That's the going rate."

Yet, what readers might well remember most vividly from this book is its unflinching account of the sheer repulsiveness of camp life. None of this is for the squeamish. But Debreczeni is insistent that we understand what life is like for people denied the fundamentals of human existence: to eat, to drink, to wash.

Disease and lice are everywhere. "Our blankets are swarming with silvery-glistening colonies of larvae." Underwear is a rare treasure. If you have it, you look after it, like the man who, using a needle, "strove tirelessly to exterminate the lice larvae from under the hems of [his] underpants." There is no sanitation. "Every couple of minutes we move over and squat, emptying pus. Bouts of diarrhea afflict some men twenty times a day."

Debreczeni's voyage into hell ends in a hospital camp, maintained because, as the Allies approached, the Nazis feared being caught red-handed engaged in obvious mass murder. There the living bunk up alongside the dead and dying. Those confined to "bed" share it with men who, in the last seconds of life, involuntarily empty their bowels. Sometimes the surviving inmates prop up the corpse to look as if it is still alive: that way they might receive the dead man's food ration:

"The 'pot' is a dented tin bucket into which those who can't get up relieve themselves—assuming it reaches them in time. Those who carry the pots are usually deaf to the wailing cries urging them to come. The bucket nearly always arrives late, and the bedridden person either soils himself or, more often, does his business on the floor. Everyone has diarrhea. Hence the horrid yellow streams along the rows of beds."

These are people treated like animals who, sooner than you might expect, behave like animals. Debreczeni notices the transformation early, during that fetid, starved, parched journey in the cattle trucks, when the Nazis put their Jewish captives on "four legs" for the first time. On arrival in the Auschwitz main camp, just after they have had all their body hair shaved off, a guard shrieks an order:

"'Open your snouts!'

We understood all too well: not mouths, but snouts."

Debreczeni is a writer so, naturally, he notices that the first step toward dehumanization is taken through language. Unsentimentally, he records that this loss of humanity was an internal process as well as an external one: shorn of their clothes, their possessions, their hair, their name, prisoners ceased to be who they were, even to themselves. In the subcamp of Fürstenstein, a fellow inmate introduces himself: "'My name was Farkas. Dr. Farkas.'" The past tense of that sentence lingers.

Indeed, it comes as a jolt each time the author reminds you that these feral beings were once people, with individual lives— that the slave who just dropped dead in front of Debreczeni was, back home, known for the "provincial elegance" of his dress, that the man who speaks with now-dead loved ones in his sleep was "a wholesaler," back when they all lived on Planet Earth. The recollection of these small details is an act of defiance in itself, an insistence on restoring the humanity of those forcibly deprived of it.

Again and again come observations both poignant and ar-resting. The author tells us that when people are reduced to skin and bone, their only drive is for sustenance. "The body can have only one desire: to eat . . . There is no sexuality in the Land of Auschwitz." That's only in part down to hunger. It is also because prisoners who have inhabited "a chamber of horrors full of sores and boils oozing disgust" have come to be repelled by the human body itself.

And we learn of an urge rarely discussed, given that readers are presumed to prefer uplifting stories of survival that testify to the resilience of the human spirit. Candidly, Debreczeni notes, repeatedly, the descent into madness of those around him and the lure of suicide. "One day you suddenly imagine death to be like some sumptuous, refreshing steam bath," one prisoner says. The author himself confesses that "the thought of imminent death [has] become outright desirable."

This is an account of grinding pain and wicked barbarity, but it is punctuated by moments of intense drama. In Eule, the ultimate kapo, the dreaded "elder" of the camp, is a man named Max. One day, it falls to him to read out a list of two thousand people—by number, not name—who are to stand in a separate column. It takes him a full two hours, number after number, as each man identified trembles with fear. "Max reads out the numbers in a booming voice. All at once he happens upon his own. He must call that out, too; there's no appeal." The "camp god" has selected himself.

Debreczeni knows how incredible, in the literal sense, all this is. In the Auschwitz main camp, a fellow prisoner from France points out the chimneys, spewing out the "filthy smoke" of mass murder. "If one day someone writes about what is happening over there, they'll be seen as either crazy or as a perverse liar," the man says. Like several of those trapped by the Nazi killing machine, Debreczeni understood at the time that, in the future, there would be those whose response to the Holocaust would be to deny such horror ever happened. This painful, absorbing book is an unanswerable reply.

—Jonathan Freedland

Part I

I

—

THE LONG TRAIN, COMPRISED OF LOW BOXCARS WITH German insignia, was grinding to a halt.

"We're stopping," the word spread among the barely conscious, listless crowd.

We suspected that we were nearing our destination. We'd been herded aboard two and a half days earlier in Bačka Topola, and since then we'd stopped just twice, and only for a minute or two. On the first such occasion, some sort of thin soup was handed in through a gap wide enough to fit only the bowl containing it. The second time, the train slowed down along the open tracks. The bolts screeched open, and the German military police, in grass-green uniforms, barked shrilly:

"*Aussteigen! Zur seite! Los! Los!* [Exit! To the side! Come on! Come on!]"

We stopped by an embankment awash with flowers and beside a little patch of woods. Who could say where we were? In Hungary, Slovakia, or perhaps Poland? The henchmen, in their grass-green uniforms, announced that we could relieve ourselves.

"Going into the woods is prohibited! We will shoot at every suspicious movement!"

Hundreds upon hundreds of people stampeded toward the

designated narrow space. Old women's fading eyes were grotesque mirrors of terror. Six days earlier, these women had been
sitting in their lovely old armchairs talking of Sunday lunch.
They'd been listening to the radio and looking out at their yards
from the living rooms of their provincial homes, awaiting news
of grandchildren away on forced labor service.

Younger, married women. Days earlier they'd been sprinkling
their bosoms and arms all over with eau de toilette, and dis-
creetly draping their skirts over their knees each time they sat
down.

Girls. Fifteen, sixteen, seventeen years old. They'd learned to
curtsey properly. At home they'd left schoolbooks; perhaps a
few timid love letters in ribbon-tied, paper lace–adorned boxes
of chocolate; and wildflowers pressed between the pages of
keepsake albums.

Men. Young and old. Wide-eyed schoolboys and disheveled
adolescents. Grown-ups in their prime, men getting on in years,
octogenarians. They run; they run. For two days they had no
way of relieving themselves. They spread their legs instinctively,
squatting like animals. Urine collects in pools. Nearby, the camp
guards, in spick-and-span grass-green uniforms, don't take their
eyes off them. Not a line stirs on the faces of these guards. They
aren't human. Nor, any longer, are those who are squatting.

I believe that somewhere in Eastern Europe an extraordinary
metamorphosis took place at the edge of a verdant forest along
a railway embankment. That is where the people of this tightly
locked train of hell were transformed into animals. Just like all
the others, the hundreds of thousands of people that the madness had sent spewing out of fifteen countries toward factories
of death and gas chambers.

At that moment they put us on all four legs for the first time.

* * *

The train is slowing. . . .

What remains of life stirs in the darkness of the train cars. Of the sixty human beings herded into our boxcar back in Topola, fifty-six still show faint signs of life. Primal terror, hunger, thirst, and lack of air have already done in four of us. Their corpses have been heaped into a pile in a corner. Most of us are from the southern and central Bačka region of Serbia's Vojvodina. Mr. Mandel, the old carpenter, a good friend of my father, was among them, and he was the first to fall. Mr. Mandel had made the furniture for more than a few girls from Bačka for their betrothals. He did so always reliably, honorably.

What the old carpenter died of, I think, was that his cigarettes had been taken away. For sixty years he'd smoked fifty a day. Not a man alive had ever seen Mr. Mandel without a smoldering cigarette. His supply, along with his jewelry and money, had been confiscated back in the camp in Topola. For twenty-four hours en route, Mr. Mandel just stared blankly, stubbornly, deliriously, at the surging mass of people all around, at the billowing of all those stinking, steaming human bodies. Sixty years of work had stained his hands to a mahogany hue. On the train his right hand sometimes moved mechanically, as if holding a cigarette. Between his index and middle fingers Mr. Mandel raised the imagined cigarette to wilted lips. Like a child pretending to smoke, he even pursed his lips to puff. But after Nové Zámky, that aging head of his tilted to the side. His death was not an event. Here death could no longer be an event. For a moment, Dr. Bakács from

Novi Sad, raised that haggard head above the frayed fur vest. He gave a tired wave of the hand. Dr. Bakács was already in a bad way, too. Perhaps he was thinking that in twelve hours some other doctor in the car would be taking note of his own death.

Two people went mad. They raged incessantly for many hours. Bloodshot eyes bulged from their waxlike faces as they sprayed foamy spit all over and tried clawing at the faces and scratching at the eyes of those standing nearby. Without further ado, the camp guards shoved these two and those rounded up from the other boxcars into the woods when we stopped to relieve ourselves. A few minutes later we heard the crackle of machine-gun fire. One of the grass-green henchmen let out a thick, vile guffaw, and spat.

No, we didn't look at each other. We'd been on the road too long for that.

On the road . . . to where?

I was somehow amazed at myself. This road . . . Subotica, Budapest, Nové Zámky. *Lo and behold, I'm still alive, and I haven't gone mad, either*—so came the fleeting thought. Not that I was thinking much. To be thinking, I too—no matter how much I'd managed to hold myself together—would have needed cigarettes. And yet I had none.

Lake Balaton, frothing a restless green, comes into view through the tiny cell window of the car. On this windy, rainy first of May, tonguelike waves vomit with revulsion toward the train. I see Nagykanizsa. We rumble past the small city without stopping, though back in Topola policeman number 6626 said we'd be brought here to work.

"Have no fear," 6626 had whispered to us. "You're off to Nagykanizsa, where you'll do agricultural work."

Number 6626 was an amiable, sober-minded Hungarian peasant. He bellowed loudly at the internees loitering about in the yard, hauling stewpots, drawing water from the well, or standing about exhaustedly, but meanwhile—when the German guard wasn't looking—he winked at us blithely, wagging his head, like some chummy little rascal.

It was May 1944, and by then few Hungarian peasants were still so beguiled by Nazism that they couldn't see this much: Döme Sztójay, László Baky, László Endre, Béla Imrédy—pro-fascist Hungarian leaders—and other such murderers had lost the game. Someone would have to pay for the blood, the tears, and the kicks.

Number 6626 was mistaken all the same. We didn't go to Nagykanizsa.

The mirror of the Drava River sparkles meaninglessly upon us. On the other side is Pavelić's Nazified Croatia. That is, death. Just like that, from the middle of life. I wave my hand as did my onetime teacher of Greek, Mr. Lendvai, from the window of his faculty office ten days earlier in Sombor, as we were being loaded onto trucks on the street below, in front of the high school. I'm standing on the bed of the truck, wearing a backpack and a jacket with a homemade, regulation-size yellow star. Mr. Lendvai, whose class I finished in 1924 with an A, and the other teachers look out numbly at the truck and its anxious throng of passengers. Our eyes meet, and Mr. Lendvai waves his hand just so. I understood.

The world is over. Everything is over. So said Mr. Lendvai's wave of the hand.

Nenikekas Judaiae . . . nenikekas Judaiae . . . Wretched Jews . . . wretched Jews . . .

* * *

The prisoners walk on the sprawling grounds of the Topola internment camp. Older folks dodder along, hands clasped behind their backs. Some people exchange tearful smiles on recognizing each other. Present here is practically the entire team of Yugoslavia's onetime Hungarian-language daily paper: editors and other staff, old and new. Our cynicism masks our despair.

"The women and children were rounded up yesterday," says stumpy Lajos Jávor, who suffers from heart trouble. His bloodless lips are wincing strangely even though his perpetual smile is frozen on his face. "In Subotica, Sombor, Novi Sad. Everywhere. They rounded up everyone."

Dr. János Móricz, the onetime editor in chief, to whom I'd once handed over my first pieces, in anxious veneration, wipes his pince-nez spectacles and snaps at me:

"Translate this to Hungarian if you're a translator."

Hopelessness takes off all its clothes in everyone's eyes. Damp, frayed straw mattresses lie about within the ugly, red-stone building. The persecuted sit on heaps of suitcases and rucksacks, staring blankly ahead. A few of them still have cigarettes, which they managed to hide from the guards on arrival. They are now prodigal smokers. No one here bothers with tomorrow. Nor even with the next fifteen minutes. Despair doesn't look through calendars, and it pays no heed to planning. Tomorrow is shrouded in a fog of distance so hopeless that it might as well be the next millennium, when people might be wandering about in skirts or tunics, when there won't be relocation camps and, perhaps, the guiltless need not be punished.

Tomorrow . . . But who bothers with that? After all, even the women were rounded up yesterday. As were the children. But why? Almighty madness, why? We don't dare think through the thought. There, in Topola, few of us had heard of Auschwitz, and little at that. Vague snippets of information about the chilling terrors of the Polish ghettos had reached us, true, and with chattering teeth we can recall the deportation of women from Slovakia, but only yesterday all this was distant and unbelievable. Not even now did we dare think seriously that we would be hauled away, abroad, thousands and thousands of innocents. We tried cheering up ourselves and the others by concocting technical difficulties.

"The Nazis now have other problems. Where would they acquire the coal, boxcars, trains, and people needed to pull off this sort of mass migration?"

So said Béla Maurer, lawyer and political commentator, in a tone of voice tolerating no dissent. Indeed, the others' expressions were encouraging. Hungarian workers and peasants had not yet been irrevocably clouded in their thinking by the madness of the brownshirts. They sensed instinctively that the folks in charge had lead in their wings. The more intrepid among them mouthed off in taverns about villainous things going on. They were already smiling at the flowery communiqués from the front, at constrained euphemisms such as "breakaway military maneuvers," "strategic retreats," "redeployments," and "repositioning."

On Hungarian land, smug Germans were already being showered with dark glances. The people could see what their leaders didn't want to see: the tired, rumpled, unshaven Wehrmacht regulars; the imbecilic, apathetic SS guards, whose merciless eyes had already sunk deep under their helmets; the ditzy fifteen- and sixteen-year-old kids draped in shirts made of tent canvas—the army with which the German "allies" had occupied the country. They saw they had to go back, and they knew there was no going back. Empty streets, shuttered windows, defiantly sullen faces. The awaiting silence of the inevitable horror skulked in the villages of the Bačka region, too. The quiet of the coming storm stood on tiptoes.

When we set off on the four-kilometer march from the grounds of the camp in Topola toward the railway station, none of us—not the men with their bundles and backpacks, not the waddling kids, not the tired women—knew about Auschwitz. But the bayonet-adorned Hungarian policemen the Germans had positioned every fifty meters along the road, they knew.

Hatred smoldered in the eyes of the policemen. That carefully seeded hatred whose proxies, trained to follow commands, didn't exactly question a whole lot. And yet there were some whose sober-minded peasant humanity was resuscitated by the stunning scene. A few of the armed statues lining the road murmured:

"May God save you!"

The half-conscious people wobbling along don't even glance that way, but that ominous sentence of farewell is still resounding in me when, from far away, I first glimpse our train along one of the platforms at the station. The cars with their "DR" emblem—Deutsche Reichsbahn (German National Railway)—speak a German even more German than that of the German camp guards accompanying us. We're being deported, after all. The best-case scenario: gas chambers. The worst-case: slave labor until death.

And to think how sorry we'd felt for those eight among us who'd taken their own lives at the camp when the order for departure had come—when it became clear that our Hungarian camp was nothing more than a relocation site. The whole thing had been more tolerable, after all, as long as we could keep telling ourselves that they'd keep us there or order us to some other place in Hungary. Topola, Bačka . . . ! This familiar conceptual duality, this thought, had somehow kept the terror of utter hopelessness at bay. Topola was still a bit of home.

Our eyes sought hope, and glinting before them was the dubious, if not yet completely discredited, promise of personal security represented by the four numbers gleaming on the belts of the Hungarian Royal Gendarmes. Grasping at the straws of a familiar landscape, we held out hope that we were not yet completely outside the law of our land. A Hungarian Nazi could be just as cruel as a German one. He could be just as determined. But his ingenuity—so we felt—had not yet warped into the sadism of the gas chambers.

2

T HE TRAIN SLOWS DOWN.
We scramble to crane our necks by the tiny window
with iron bars. Once again, that window has become interest-
ing. In the past twenty-four hours we've hardly glanced out of
it. What could there have been worth seeing? Rubinfeld alone
looked out now and again.

Rubinfeld wound up in our car two nights ago amid exceptional circumstances. The train had slowed then, too, before
stopping with a jolt. The car door suddenly tore open, and unfamiliar hands shoved in a man covered with blood. We then
started off at once. Obviously, we'd stopped for this reason
alone. Around dawn a smidgen of light filtered in, and a few
of us recognized Rubinfeld. A Jewish refugee from L'viv, he was
one of the thousands of unfortunates Hitler's expansion had
driven from their homes and chased across half of Europe. In
the course of his ordeal, he'd traveled through Vienna, Prague,
Warsaw, Belgrade, and Budapest. So it was that he'd wound up
in Bačka. There he lived, or, rather, he'd been hiding, for a good
few months in Novi Sad. He was partly toying with, and partly
paying off, the detectives charged with checking on foreigners.

It took two hours for him to come to and be able to tell

us what had happened. In Topola the Germans had designated a *Wagenälteste*—a Wagon Elder—for each railcar. The induction unfolded when the German guards would scream at the trembling internee nearest at hand:

"Stinking Jew, you will be the Wagenälteste!" They added, in tones of voice fit for training dogs, "So, what will you be, stinking Jew?"

"A Wagenälteste."

"That's right. Know what that is?"

"No."

"Well, I'll explain it," said the grass-green guard convivially. "The Wagenälteste answers with his head for every stinking Jew in the carriage. If one of them escapes during the trip, we'll shoot you right away. *Ist es jetzt klar* [Is this now clear]?"

"*Jawohl* [Yes, sir]!" faltered the poor wretch.

In our carriage the recipient of the fatal "honor" was Sonnenthal, the old broker suffering from advanced arteriosclerosis. Even back home the poor fellow had hardly any life in him, but he just happened to be standing closest to the door when the grass-green guard stormed in and "appointed" him. Sonnenthal did not argue. He was content to pass his teary eyes pleadingly over us and stammer:

"None of you will do anything foolish, right? Because then . . . you know . . . I'm the one they'll shoot."

Indeed, in our carriage no one did anything "foolish." After all, escape was possible by but a single means and that meant almost certain death. If someone had pried open the grate over the tiny square, head-high window and was spindly enough for such an endeavor, perhaps he could have squeezed his body through the narrow gap. Theoretically, then, it was possible for a human being to leave this hell as it hurled along the tracks. What would have probably happened then is obvious, since a planned jump would have been out of the question. Everything would have depended on the angle of the hopeless plummeting leap and what ground lay below. In our carriage no one tried, but in the one where Rubinfeld was the Wagenälteste a sixteen-year-old boy did so in the delirium of fear. To pry open the grate, he used those few minutes of the night when silence had fallen in the carriage, when numbness had taken hold of everyone. He knew that the others would have stopped him if they had noticed. The plan succeeded: the kid wriggled himself through. But the lookout in the sentries' carriage at the front of the train saw the leap.

A sharp, short whistle cut through the roar and rumble of the train, which stopped for a minute. The sentries jumped off, and within a few moments they determined that the fugitive had smashed himself to death on the shards of the steep embankment. Then they tore into Rubinfeld's carriage.

"Where's the Wagenälteste?" one of them shrieked.

Rubinfeld stepped forward, pale as a ghost.

"You all heard the order. In a car where there has been an escape attempt, we'll shoot the Wagenälteste. To hell with you, you rotten Jew! Shoot him! Ahead!"

Rubinfeld was dragged out. The clatter of machine-gun fire in the night, and then, once again, the train's whistle. We'd started off.

The others in Rubinfeld's carriage had thought their Wagenälteste was dead. In a sudden rush of magnanimity—perhaps brought on by the sight of the child's shattered body on the rocks of that embankment—the sentries had shot into the air, not at Rubinfeld. The guards dragged the victim to their own carriage and were then content to beat him unconscious with the butts of their rifles. They then sent the motionless body flying into the nearest car, which happened to be ours.

So it was that this Polish Jew with sad eyes wound up among us. It took hours for us to get him to come to. We had cotton, rolls of gauze, and antiseptic. We bandaged up his beaten-in skull, which was covered by a sparse layer of gray hair matted down with clotted blood.

So it was that in the remaining part of the journey Rubinfeld became our guide, our chief source of information, our prophet. Unfortunately, he was all too much a prophet in his native land. He knew the countryside like the palm of his hand. Back in peacetime he'd traveled here on countless occasions for business trips; he was familiar with every railway line and junction, as well as salient features of the natural and human landscape. Whenever the train passed the many switches that it did and the wheels' characteristic click-clack signaled a station, Rubinfeld arose, dragged his feet to the window, and stared into the night.

"It's still not certain which way they're taking us," he kept saying at first. "Sixty to eighty kilometers ahead the line branches two ways."

He mentioned lots of Polish station names heavy on consonants.

"For now, a short detour could mean either Austria, Germany, or even Poland."

"But it doesn't matter, huh?" someone said with a sigh, with nods all around.

Rubinfeld replied emphatically:

"Yes. It sure does. Austria means life. There we'd have a

chance of getting through this. We could wind up doing agricultural work. The Austrian peasant doesn't get brutal."

"And the Reich?"

"Lower odds there. Probably factory work. Or building railroads. Maybe cleaning up ruins in larger cities, with the constant risk of air raids. Jews can't go to shelters. Hunger. Billy clubs. No, it's hard to survive the Reich."

He fell silent. The blood had soaked through the makeshift bandage on his head.

Later we rumbled past yet more railroad switches. A fainthearted dawn glimmered its lowly light toward us through the window. The third one we'd seen on this hellish road. Rubinfeld again forced himself to his feet. We looked out. The wheels were grinding up a pair of tracks turning eastward. To the left, the blurry contours of a train station with a Polish name shrank into the distance.

The old man sat back down in his rabbit hole without looking at a soul.

"Auschwitz," he said a bit later, softly, ahead of himself and to himself. "Now it's certain. This station decided it. This is where the line branches off."

There were many in our carriage who'd now heard the word for the first time. A few of us remembered having read about an American film depicting the horrors of the gas chambers. Naturally, the film had not been shown in Hungary.

Auschwitz...

Starting back in 1939, after the Polish capitulation, Rubinfeld had already experienced the ghettos. He was the only one among us who knew the details of the Nazis' gigantic factories of death. Only those standing near him could hear his broken, trailing words. Not that we were too curious in any case about the details. Soon we were to be suffering participants in what yesterday had been a foggy, distant horror.

Some cast him disbelieving stares. Even now, what information of the horrors that *had* reached those of us who'd grown up in the well-made bed of the bourgeois lifestyle seemed distant, as if read in a novel. And yet the wheels of this train of death were already click-clacking reality into this impression.

Finally, we must believe. So we've managed that, too. With surprising indifference. A few of us still have food. Not much, because while in Topola our food hadn't been confiscated, everyone had already consumed most of their meager supplies. With treachery befitting their fascist selves, the German guards, in tones of voice full of good intentions, had even cautioned their victims that forty-eight hours of food would be enough, since food would be provided at the camp. Hence more than a few of us didn't even have food at all, but what we had we shared.

That third dawn fast became a sunlit spring morning. Light panned the dark carriage, which smelled of suffering, making its way through this cell packed with the stale odor of sweating human bodies.

It was spring, but our admission to this spring, so it seemed, was no longer valid.

Later, on this third day, the train again chugged along at its usual pace. Gradually the foreboding mountains in the distance fell away behind us. We were making our way through a flat landscape reminiscent of the Bačka and the Hungarian plains.

Standing by the window once more, Rubinfeld spoke:

"We'll be in Auschwitz in a half hour."

From this point on the whole thing became like a fitful,

disquieting dream of the sort that grips you in sleep after a heavy supper. On emerald-green carpets of grass we saw beings in strange costumes, as if dressed for a carnival. They plodded along, making precise gestures reminiscent of a slow-motion film. They swayed back and forth, took small steps, stopped again and again. The men wore rags, the tattered remnants of gray, black, and blue everyday outfits; the women, dirty brown work dresses. Comically baggy pants flopped about on some. Ghosts and scarecrows. Screaming-loud yellow and red splotches of paint splattered capriciously on the outfits—on chests, legs, backs. From the train, a few hundred meters away, it seemed that they were taking affected, measured steps to the beat of a funeral march. These ghosts were doing agricultural work.

Most striking was how they were trudging along, as if carrying heavy loads.

Rubinfeld offered a better explanation.

"Deportees. These here are from Auschwitz."

"And the costumes? What about those grotesque costumes?"

"Some of them are in scrap clothes that had belonged to those murdered in the gas chambers. The paint is to make escape hard even for those who aren't wearing prison clothes. Those glaring, mottled splotches give away a *häftling*—a prisoner—from even a hundred meters away."

Before long, the train was racing by an endless display of smokestacks, warehouses, heaps of barrels, and rusty wreckage of airplanes. Stretching out black before us was a pair of tracks at a station. On the tracks next to ours was a train comprising old-fashioned passenger cars. A woman in a kerchief was leaning out of one of the cars, and we heard a bawling child. Men were standing about on the platforms, smoking cigarettes and holding toolboxes, bags, suitcases. Swaggering between the platforms was a white-capped traffic officer.

No one looked twice at us. Were we dressed so well that no one sensed that we were marked for death, or had death trains become an everyday sight by now? To this day I don't know.

The smoky brown station building now came into view before us. It differed not one bit from so many other provincial stations I'd passed by carelessly on trains so many times before in my life. On the façade and on each side was just a German-language sign, in capital letters: Auschwitz. In the "General Government" that had been Poland, there was no more town of Oświęcim.

The town, too, was visible for a moment or two. The shrill whistles of train engines called out to each other, and then, a jolt.

Nine AM. We'd arrived.

3

W E RUSH TO THE WINDOW YET AGAIN. THE CAMP GENDARMES leap from the passenger cars at the front of our train. In groups of two or three, they charge at each carriage and attack the locks. The bolts snap open with rusty creaks. The doors tear apart. Fresh sun and sweet, cool morning air pour in. I take deep, bountiful breaths. I look in my companions' sallow faces and see my own.

Auschwitz . . .

A gaunt SS officer approaches. One of the grass-green guards stands bolt upright at attention and barks out a report. The officer nods, says something, and at once the command rings out:

"Get out, with bags too! Everyone line up in front of their cars. *Los* [Come on]*!*"

The breeze goes right through me—it's been a while since I've felt one—and I squint in the morning light. The warm short lambskin jacket I'm wearing has been with me through four different labor camps. It's dependable, to be sure, and yet here I shudder all the same. Perhaps it's not the air that does this to me but waiting for the unknown. Beside me, Márkus, a man of means from Subotica, chews away stubbornly on some bread crust. He's also run out of cigars. The last pungent Virginia died out between those ever-grumbling lips before we got as far as Nové Zámky. Who knows what he was thinking? This man who for fifty years kept chasing a mirage that can be expressed in numbers: money. And now, as if he were a stray bug, the guard swatted him off the bag of treasures he had been painstakingly weaving for a long time.

Meanwhile the grass-green guards, with the help of some paint-splotched figures, throw the motionless from the cars. The veteran häftlinge work indifferently and adeptly. They fling the bodies onto handcarts—there may be living among those bodies—and then wordlessly set their shoulders to the handles.

A new command:

"Bags are to be left in front of the cars! Line up in rows of five!"

Again, the marching column we had back in Topola has taken shape, but now pared down quite a bit: there are perhaps one thousand or twelve hundred people here still able to stand on their feet.

We cast agonizing glances toward our bags. If we can't take the stuff with us, the chance of quick annihilation is even greater. If need be—so we had thought—we could trade in our blankets, warm clothes, and brand-new hobnail boots for food.

The procession began reluctantly, although a bit of encouraging news was already making the rounds, but who knows how it began:

"They're bringing the luggage on a truck behind us."

After a few hundred steps came the command to stop. A big, almost perfectly square space. Just as large as that major intersection, Oktogon, along the Grand Boulevard back in Budapest. Barracks with chimneys spewing out smoke. To the right, a yellow-and-black crossing gate closes off a well-maintained, steep road. A watchtower. A machine-pistol-toting sentry was stomping back and forth a few steps away from the wooden structure, and machine guns were yawning our way from the tower's loopholes. Fifteen or twenty trucks were all around us, with armed SS soldiers and drivers beside them. The grass-green guards who'd accompanied us from back home had vanished. On the square, in gray uniforms, SS lads, junior officers, and senior officers—the "gray ones," as I came to think of them—were strutting about.

First, the women were commanded to separate from the rest of us. They stagger and stumble along, one behind the other, numb with fear. Hundreds of people, with watery eyes, watch their wives, mothers, and daughters now fade into the distance. Mothers and daughters spasmodically clasp each other's hands as girlfriends do the same. The sparse, silvery hair of trembling old women sparkles in the sun. Mothers with babies shrieking in terror are lulling them or deliriously squeezing them to their breasts. In a sprawling, stretched-out column the women and girls now disappear forever. Moments later the barracks envelop them, but the crying of children can be heard for quite a while.

A group of four men approaches us: two officers, a tall one with gold-framed glasses and carrying a paper form, and another, toting a briefcase; and two storm troopers with icy expressions. They stop, step apart, with two on each side facing each other. We must pass between them in a line down this narrow corridor they've fashioned. The man with the form in his hand glances at everyone and gives a wave of his hand. Right or left. The other three drive the victims accordingly in the direction indicated.

Right or left. To a life of slavery or to death in the gas chamber.

Those who've made it home know what it meant if someone went left. But, then, we didn't know yet. The decisive moment slunk away, unnoticed, amid the others.

The gray-haired, the emaciated, the nearsighted, and the lame mostly go to the left. So that's the "medical exam." In a half hour two almost identically long lines of people, five to a row, form on the right and the left. The four Germans consult briefly, whereupon one of them steps between the two groups.

"There will now be a ten-kilometer march uphill to the camp. You"—and he points to the left—"older and weaker ones will go by truck, the others on foot. Anyone among those on the right who doesn't feel strong enough to walk can step over to the left."

Long, heavy moments of silence. The condemned and their executioners stare at each other. The announcement, issued in such a detached, natural-sounding voice, doesn't spark a bit of suspicion. Only a few of us are flummoxed by the generosity. This is not the Nazis' style. Many prepare to go all the same. Even I make an involuntary movement. That's when one of the carts carrying the dead turns closer to us. It rattles past between the two columns a few steps away. The häftling beside the shoulder bar does not look at us, but I can hear his subdued voice:

"*Hier blieben! Nur zu Fuss! Nur zu Fuss!* [Stay here! Only on foot! Only on foot!]"

He says it several times, but few of us hear this stranger's lifesaving warning. I decide. I'm scared of the journey on foot, and yet I stay. It's more that I obey some instinct that suddenly flares up in me rather than the comrade pulling the handcart. I grab the arm of my neighbor, Pista Frank.

"Don't go over," I whisper.

Nervously he tears himself from my grip and heads off. Others too. The line thins out noticeably. The gray ones smile slyly, whisper among themselves, point toward us. Once those who've opted to go have gone, our group is surrounded by two platoons holding bayonets up high. We're off.

Those on the left are still standing there. We pass by them closely indeed. There is Horovitz, the sickly old photographer; Pongrác, the wheat farmer; and Master Lefkovits, whose prestigious long-standing men's clothing store on Main Street had supplied so many of the fancy silk neckties and shirts of my twenties youth; Weisz, the lame bookseller; Porzács, the morbidly obese jazz pianist, who in Subotica's most fashionable café popularized the latest hits with boundless ambition if with deficient technical aptitude. There, with the corners of his mouth turned down, looking withered, and with six days of white stubble, was Waldmann, who taught Hungarian and German literature in the "Royal Hungarian" high school in my hometown. Hertelendi, the half-witted midget, Samu, whom everyone called a war simpleton, though no one knew why. Here was Kardos, the lawyer from Szeged with heart trouble. He was my age, and we'd met four times already when forced into labor service. A notorious slacker, he always managed to dodge the work. Most recently this was our jocular farewell, at the camp in Hódmezővásárhely: "Until we don't see each other again at labor service." Now here he was, standing in that outrageous yellow corduroy "enlistment outfit" of his, as he called it. This is what he always wore; he'd gotten it on even for the most recent enlistment. His eyes sparkle snidely from behind his horn-rimmed glasses as he stares at our group. He clearly believes that even now he chose the better option. Why, he won't even be walking the ten kilometers!

And here are the rest of us. I glance at faces familiar and unfamiliar. Acquaintances and semi-acquaintances—ten, one hundred, five hundred. . . . The engines of the waiting trucks have already started up. The crossing gate, painted red, white, and black, rises before us, and we turn down the sloping asphalt road, which is lined with barracks. The watchtower's machine guns turn slowly toward us.

As for them, those on the left, no one saw them ever again.

* * *

The bayonet-toting guards in front of us, behind, and to our sides command a labored pace. Why the hurry? One thing is already clear: we won't ever again be seeing the bags we left by the boxcars. This too is the Nazi way of doing things: it's much simpler to lift a person out of his property than to take property away from a person. The procedure is more expedient and—most important—means less dotting of i's and crossing of t's, fewer formalities, and less administration. The Nazis' Hungarian disciples sweated away taking notes, making lists, and keeping records as they carried out such pillaging. The Nazis had long ago simplified the matter.

We pass by an endless row of defunct wooden buildings. The fast march is exhausting; I gasp for breath and the nippy air makes me dizzy. Eventually we see people. Prisoners are moving about in blue-striped gray linen outfits beside droning cement mixers in yards fenced off with bars and barbed wire. Unmatched pairs of wooden shoes are clapping away, wounded toes peering out. I don't imagine, I don't want to imagine, that in a couple hours we too will be commanded to remove the last memory of home: the clothes on our bodies.

On a huge field surrounded by barbed wire is a heap of airplane wreckage. The planes' rusty frames are protruding skyward, and dangling from them are the threadbare, scorched outer layers. German, Russian, British, and American insignia are on the remains of the wings. This airplane cemetery, here, of all places, is frightful and distressing. Between the barracks, lumpy, clay-filled yellow potato fields. Hardly a human being is to be seen. For a half hour straight our escorts' impatient prodding voices are the only sound:

"*Los, los* [Come on, come on]*!*"

Then, rails; and then barracks yet again. This time, multistory structures. One of them has a wooden board on it: Häftling Krankenhaus [Prisoner Hospital]. Before it, a häftling with his arm in a sling gapes at our column as we go by. We barely notice that we're now on a busy road.

We've arrived in Auschwitz, in whose wooden buildings hundreds of thousands of deportees from every corner of Europe have been crammed by those running amok with racial madness.

Busy intersections, directional signs. Block No. XXI, says one. Busy people, carts, and cars—every external aspect of a city's milieu, but buildings of wood, not stone, and instead of people, skeletons wobbling along in striped sackcloth uniforms. Instead of streets, "blocks," meaning one or more groups of barracks under joint command.

The skeleton-people are carrying beams, crates, and barrels, and pushing handcarts. Trucks lurch forward one after another from the adjacent streets. The whole scene is like a grotesque parody.

On one corner we come face-to-face with sackcloth figures grunting with exertion in unison while hauling rails. They need to stop on the narrow street to let us pass. They show no great surprise on seeing us, though we do on seeing them. They call out to us in Hungarian.

"So, not even you folks managed to wind up in a better place," one of them calls out with contemptuous compassion.

A cacophony of shouts showers down on us:

"Drop your grub!"... "Cigarettes, combs, knives!"... "Who's got grub? Quickly!"... "Cigarettes, cigarettes!"... "Aren't any of you from Košice?"... "From Oradea!"... "Lučenec!"... "Anyone from Budapest?! Budapest?!"... "What's the news from home?"... "Grub!... Quickly!... Drop it!"... "Food, food!"... "Morons, you'll turn in everything at the showers, anyway!"

In shock, we stare idiotically at those who are shouting. An SS soldier approaches: the rail carriers fall silent, and we go on.

"Halt!" comes the command.

We come to a sudden, disorderly stop by a long, one-story barrack at the end of the street. The sign on its façade proclaims: Schreibenstube [Clerk's Office].

A few häftlinge step in front of us. Their movements are self-assured; their striped costumes, spick-and-span. They are wearing freshly polished, handsome oxfords. Sewn to the chest of each of their uniforms is a triangle of brightly colored fabric. Below it, a tiny, chrome-plated tag engraved with four numbers. The embroidered letters on their sky-blue armbands have an ornamental flourish, as on a home blessing, and spell: *Blockälteste* [Block Elder].

Each and every Blockälteste is a bundle of haughtiness and domineering self-assurance through and through. On the outside, they are deportees just the same as the others. But only on the outside.

This was my first encounter with the bigwigs: the camp aristocracy, the wretched gods of this wretched world.

* * *

And let me say right away what I didn't know then but later, through fourteen months, witnessed with such numb, never exactly conscious awe. With systematic resourcefulness the Nazis created in their death camps a subtle hierarchy of the pariahs. The Germans themselves remained mostly invisible behind the barbed wire. The allocation of food, the discipline, the direct supervision of work, and the first degree of terror—in sum, executive power—were in fact entrusted to slave drivers chosen randomly from among the deportees.

A profound psychology undeniably lay hidden in the system. Those who dreamt it up knew the layers of instinct of the psyche. For their hideous work, the slave drivers the Germans appointed from among the prisoners received, in addition to better soup, better clothes, and the opportunity to steal, power itself, that most intoxicating opiate of all. Boundless power over life and death. They created a long and varied system of positions, essentially the same ones in all the camps, always attending carefully to the hierarchy. The camp officers and the noncommissioned officers: the bosses invariably came from those transports that arrived first in this or that completed camp or at a yet-to-be-built campsite.

The SS sergeant or corporal commanding the camp or the site would single out a slave:

"You'll be the *Lagerälteste* [the Camp Elder]."

Another prisoner would be "appointed" camp clerk. These two then saw to the rest. They named the other officers from among their relatives, friends, and acquaintances. So it was that most often the häftlinge comprising the whole of the so-called camp staff were from the same region or even the same town. Only privates could be recruited from transports arriving later.

At the bottom rung of the ladder of prisoner functionaries were the junior *kapos*. Each one led a ten-to-fifteen-member work crew at the work sites of private companies engaged in construction work and leasing slaves. The company would pay the Nazi state two or two and a half marks per slave. The junior kapo's duty was to drive the häftling—with the help of the civilian foreman, or *Meister*, and the SS guard, the so-called *Posten*—with a cudgel, a whip, or sometimes an iron rod. He generally carried this out like a "real man," since if he came off as more tender-hearted or indulgent than what was expected of him the Meister would unceremoniously beat him and demote him. And this meant the end of immunity from work murderous to body and soul, the end of a greater chance than the others to survive the hell.

And yet the junior kapo could not count himself as belonging to the exclusive club of camp royalty. He slept in the common quarters for prisoners, and he had to stand in line for soup just like everyone. And yet, instead of a spade, a shovel, or a sledgehammer, his hand held a whip.

Towering above him in rank like Mount Olympus were the first- and second-rank kapos at the companies. These had privileges carrying full membership and titles. They were at home in the company offices. There they received the list of daily tasks. Their official responsibility was to take a count during the *Appell*, or roll call, each morning at dawn of the team of five or six hundred men assigned to the company, and, along with the SS sentries, herd them to the distribution center. There the Meister and the junior kapos were waiting for them. They formed the crews that then headed off to the work sites that were usually several kilometers away.

The company kapos had ample opportunity to curry favor from the company's work supervisors, and perhaps with Todt's people—the engineers and others associated with Fritz Todt.* Something or other might "drop" here and there: cigar butts in the ashtrays in the company offices, the odd glass of brandy, wine, or beer, and even whole packages of tobacco, bread, and clothing turned up at times.

This was an important rank not only because of the power that came with it but also because it was accompanied by all those advantages ensured by a greater freedom and sphere of movement and frequent contact with the world beyond the barbed wire. Within the camp, the company kapo was among the closest associates of the Lagerälteste, the god of all gods. He got some of the better-quality soup cooked in a separate cauldron for the aristocracy, and shared in the substantial quantity of foodstuffs stolen during the distribution of rations: sugar, margarine, jam, artificial honey, cheese, and, especially, bread, which meant life. It's easy to imagine what quantities could be "put aside" every day from among the rations of two or three thousand men, what

---

* The top Nazi who had instituted the slave labor operations in the camps.

could be nabbed from the huge crates and barrels that arrived. All this was managed behind strictly locked doors by the *Älteste*—the elder, or commander—and those around him. At the hospital camp in Dörnhau, I saw three big sacks of sugar, many crates of margarine, and hundreds upon hundreds of cans of meat piled up in the Lagerälteste's sanctuary.

Four or five private companies contracted with most camps, and yet the number of company kapos was rather large. Each kapo kept two or three orderlies, usually fourteen- or fifteen-year-old kids. Even being an office boy signified a certain rank. Adorning a company kapo's immaculate armband were the company name and the kapo's rank. For example, to the häftling, the inscription "KAPO I. G. URBAN TIEF-UND HOCHBRAU A. G." meant he was face-to-face with the Urban Company's head kapo, and he'd be wise to snap off his brimless round inmate's cap.

Being a *Lagerkapo*, or camp kapo, was an honor equal to that of being a company kapo. The Lagerkapo was the adjunct of the Älteste and the commander of those häftlinge who toiled not at workplaces outside the barbed wire but within the camp. Mainly the camp tradesmen: cobblers, barbers, woodworkers, carpenters, locksmiths, and repairmen. He also supervised another privileged class—kitchen workers, potato peelers, and furnace cleaners—though each such group had its own kapo, a position that likewise signified unearthly might. The *Schäler-kapo*, the commander of the potato peelers, was the first among equals. As with the commander of the Noble Guard that once served the Pope, he commanded a crew of men, each of whom was himself a de facto officer. Potato peels were closely guarded, sought-after treasures, too; and potatoes were life itself, like bread. Yes, to work in the proximity of potatoes, to work *with* potatoes, and, more generally, to go near the kitchen, was itself a rank and a cherished privilege.

Independent of the Lagerkapo but in an even more dignified position was the Blockälteste, the all-powerful ruler of the block. The block comprised twenty to thirty twenty-four-person acid-green-painted wood-frame tents; or, in camps where the deportees had already built the barracks, it was a wooden building housing five or six hundred men.

The Lagerälteste had his very own room and crew of servants, which signified his power. He too could put aside a good store of supplies, because after imposing his own toll on the wretched "allowances," he handed out the remainder in one unit to the block. The Blockälteste doled out some of that to his own people. Without a drop of shame, he thus cut the calories allotted to each of us, which had been determined precisely to be sufficient to merely keep us alive.

Two kapos alone ruled above the Blockälteste: the Lagerälteste and the camp clerk, the Lagerschreiber. These two positions were officially of the same rank at every camp, without exception. Who carried more weight, which one became more festooned and more dreaded, depended on their personalities. In some camps, the clerk represented the more fearsome authority; elsewhere, the Lagerälteste. There were even some camps with a deputy Lagerälteste, or else the clerk surrounded himself with five or six deputies. Again, each of these could count on having power in his hands. The clerk and the Lagerälteste were high enough in rank everywhere to raise up their relatives, friends, and favorites to the footstools beside their thrones.

The second branch of the camp aristocracy comprised the kitchen workers; and the third, doctors and other health-care staff. Their castes became more tangled, fissured, and sprouted foliage and side branches, especially in those factories of death ludicrously dubbed hospital camps. Those were swarming with camp head doctors, doctors who oversaw the camp clinic, block head doctors, and head "medics," as well as the deputies of all these top medical staff and the deputies' deputies. Each one had real power; each had unlimited authority over one or many people they could murder without a consequence in the world, whose guts they could stamp out, whose eyes they could gouge out, and whose flesh they could whip right off their bare backs.

This aristocratic hierarchy reflected the Nazis' modern interpretation of the concept "divide and conquer." The sadistic madness that now prevailed brought this distorted concept to fruition in the Land of Auschwitz, in this phantom country that stank of excrement, this country whose border station, the clerk's building, we now stood before.

4

—

THOSE WITH THE BLOCKÄLTESTE ARMBANDS ARE SPEAKING
Polish with each other. But they scream at us with labored,
Slavic-accented German.

"To the office in groups of three! Identity check!"

One of them notices that a few of us are sitting, exhausted,
on the ground. Like wild animals they charge at the terrified
group and whack a few dumbfounded faces with their rubber
truncheons. Those hit scream out in pain, bloody, while the rest
of us stare numbly.

"Stand up, filthy gang of Jews! Where do you think you are?
Synagogue? A theater? Well, you'll find out, anyway."

This was unmistakably local color à la Auschwitz. Slaves
beating slaves. The first to be sent to the capital of the Great
Land of Auschwitz were Polish deportees, most of them not
Jews. As at all camps, here too most of the aristocracy comprised the first settlers.

And yet it's Hungarian häftlinge who are in these offices.

Unsuspectingly I ask one of them, "When did you get here?
What's the situation?"

An ice-cold, haughty stare is the reply. I take a big gulp. It
seems I dared strike up a conversation with one of the bosses.

From the office we're led to the bathhouse. While waiting, a few of us managed to get some information out of camp natives shuffling past. We now know for sure: we need to hand in what we have on us. A fast and feverish round of indulgence follows. Those with any cigarettes left light up two at once. Cigarette butts are being passed around. We quickly divvy up and start chewing the food left in our pockets.

Men with yet other armbands take command of us in front of the bathhouse. Polish Jews. Bitter moments ensue. We have to strip buck naked in the biting wind. On command we toss our clothes, shoes, and every object in our pockets onto a heap. We're still shivering there, in front of the wooden shack that is the bathhouse, when the trucks arrive. Yet others in striped uniforms toss our things aboard, and the trucks clatter on. Letters, precious photos, and a few odd personal documents we'd managed to rescue back in Topola fade irrevocably away. The short act unfolds ornately. *Lasciate ogni speranza* [Abandon all hope]! No going back from here. If there were, at least the personal effects would have been hauled away in separate packages marked with names. This way, not even if they wanted to could they return the items to their owners. Its very barbarity makes it a remarkably simple method: to deprive millions by this means of their individuality, their names, their humanity. How can I someday prove so far from home that I was called this, not that? How will I prove that I am I?

The minutes feel like hours. With ungainly, bitter smiles we study each other's nakedness, awash with goose bumps from the cold. Finally, finally, we can go into the pen. The vestibule of the bathhouse. The heavy dampness on its wooden walls sweats a hideous mildew. In a corner, a boiler oozes thick steam.

The sweating, dusty human bodies emit an excruciating stink that weighs heavily upon our chests, but the warmth caresses. The clippers are snapping away. "Barbers," naked from the waist up, are shaving all the body hairs off those in the transport that arrived before us. This is the second stage. Cutting of pubic hair, hair on heads, and underarm hair. Prophylaxis against lice. I stare with astonishment at the butchers. Is there no human solidarity in them at all?

With a blunt nonchalance they hand off the victims among themselves. They shove; they pinch; they kick. With rusty, chipped clippers one of them plows the length of the under-arms; another shaves the hair off heads; and a third, off pubes and scrotums. The naked people emerge bloody and, most often, with serious, painful wounds from under the rough, bungling hands before being whirled through a door.

A häftling steps up beside me. He addresses me in broken German.

"Where are you folks from?"

"Hungary."

"What's the news from the fronts?"

Tears are welling up in his sunken, baggy eyes. His voice trembles with a pleading tone. I cordially recite a list.

"The Germans are retreating everywhere. The Russians reaped a decisive victory in Gomel. The West is preparing a land invasion. By every indication, the Finns, the Romanians, and the Bulgarians are soon opting out. It can't last much longer. Where are you from?"

"Paris."

"Merchant?"

"Lawyer."

"Have you been here long?"

"More than a year. These animals have killed all my loved ones."

"Is it possible to survive here?"

"If luck is on your side, maybe. Your chances now are in any case a year more than mine. I wasn't lucky. My lungs were weak back home, too. I won't last much longer."

He gives a dismissive wave and spits.

"You won't wind up in the gas chambers, that's for sure," he adds. "Those who get baths in this block are going to work. You'll be heading on right away, in fact. Auschwitz itself is packed to the gills, so new arrivals don't stay here. But that doesn't matter. It's the same in all the subcamps."

"What's a subcamp?"

He points all around.

"This is a whole country here. Everywhere around us, four or five kilometers from each other, hundreds of men's and women's camps have been built or are being built. Auschwitz itself is just a hub. The capital. It's not even the only one in this region. The other is called Gross-Rosen. There are many such camp nations out there."

"Beside the train they divided us into two groups. The others had to go by truck. You haven't seen them?"

A singular, agonized smile comes over his sunken face.

"Was the other group lined up on the left?"

"Yes. We were told they'd get to ride on trucks."

This man in a striped uniform raises one of his thin hands and points into the distance.

"See those chimneys there? That's Birkenau. The crematorium city. The smoke there is already—them. Those who stood
to the left."

Yes, perhaps I was even prepared for something like this.
Even back home I'd heard and read plenty of ghoulish stories
about gas chambers and crematoriums. But this is different. Not
hearsay. Not something read. Not a distant threat, but a reality
rearing up right in front of me. A nearby reality. It can't be
even two hundred meters away. Its smoke strikes my nostrils.
Maybe that's why I just stand there staring, petrified, at this
tuberculosis-afflicted little Frenchman.

The whole thing is beyond a doubt and yet unbelievable. An
early May day is blossoming: morning is glistening; people are
moving about; the sky is stretching with youthful vigor above
me. And yet the reality is over there: the filthy, swirling smoke
two hundred meters away.

I think of the yellow corduroy suit and sparkling eyeglasses
of Kardos, that fellow from Szeged with heart trouble; of Weisz,
the lame bookseller; of my teacher Waldmann; and of the rest,
who, back there, on that rectangular square, in the shadow of
machine-gun towers and SS soldiers smiling slyly, stood waiting
for trucks. Not quite four hours earlier.

The Frenchman stares at the ground. Ferreting out a crum-
pled cigarette from his pocket, he peels away the paper and removes the tobacco with boundless care. He divides the paper in
two, stuffs each piece with the tobacco, and rolls them into thin
stubs. He extends one to me. I am filled with deep, warm gratitude, for I've already come to realize what a treasure tobacco is
here. Silently I squeeze his hand. We both turn away from the
sight of the billowing cloud of smoke.

He takes a deep, wheezing sniff.

"Those chimneys spew that filthy smoke day and night," he says slowly and quietly. "A large-scale industry. If one day some- one writes about what is happening over there, they'll be seen as either crazy or a perverse liar. You need only imagine: For months, for years, day in and day out, tightly locked trains from all over Europe have been pouring in here by the hour. They have those passengers who are still alive line up on that square of death in front of the station. As with all of you. Maybe, probably, at this moment others are already standing in the very same place. At a glance, they sort those who seem weak and old, and send them to the left. Then they announce that vile tale about the trucks. As for those who fall for it, they can only blame themselves—if you make your bed you've got to lie on it."

His voice has trailed off into a whisper. He looks around. He takes a long drag on the cigarette stub, the embers glowing with rage between his bloodless lips.

"Those trucks go straight to Birkenau. It starts the same way as here: in the bathhouse. Everything unfolds with systematic, Teu- tonic planning. '*Es muss alles klappen* [Everything must work out].' It's in their blood. Panic must be avoided, so to ensue this, a verita- ble theatrical performance gets underway. Those unfortunates are first made to strip naked. Just like all of you now. They too are shaved and deloused. They think they're going to bathe. Soap is even pressed into their hands. They are pushed through a doorway and, just like everyone else, they find themselves in a shower room. But, instead of hot water, the showerheads spray gas. That's all there is to it.

"The only thing left is the crematorium," he continues. "But the trains keep running toward Germany, full of women's clothes, men's clothes, and children's clothes. And with so much else. The bones become glue; human hair is used for mattresses or pillows. There are mountains of children's hair. Krauts on Nazism to the umpteenth power. They are now in their element. Hitler knows full well what world of instincts he reaches into with his 'methods,' what layers of the subconscious are freed up in the process."

He coughs again. And spits—blood.

"I worked in Birkenau. Not in the inner zone of the crematoriums. häftlinge usually can't go near them, and if anyone is ordered in, they never come out again. Three million human bodies have so far gone up in smoke. It's a wonder the machines can keep it up." With a sarcastic tone, he adds, "Fortunately, all the complex pieces of equipment are reliable. It all comes down to the German machine industry, for as we know . . . these are the outstanding products of illustrious companies."

The cigarette stub burns down to his fingernails. At best, five strands of tobacco are left. Carefully he places the stub inside a chipped tin box. He notices that I'm trembling.

"Don't be scared," he says. "In this zone you needn't fear a thing. This is just a bathhouse, after all. And from here you'll all head right on. I know. I work here. Lots of luck!"

The Frenchman leaves. It's my turn. Tears of rage well up inside me from the butchers' harsh grips. The decrepit old clippers rip out my hair strand by strand. The guards shave us with clippers set at number 3 and plow an extra strip over the top of the head with clippers set at 0.

The fourth inquisitor shrieks:

"Open your snouts!"

We understood all too well: not mouths, but snouts.

A handheld lamp shines its strong beam into my mouth. Nazi thoroughness extends to the finest details. We're at a border station, and nothing must make it through from our old lives. After all, you can't put it past a häftling to try to smuggle a small article of gold or gemstones in his mouth—God forbid!

Finally, finally, we're in the shower room. Showerheads in long, parallel rows. We await the warm spray of water. Instead, liquid fire suddenly gushes onto our bodies. The water is unbearably hot. Screaming, we seek escape, but the hellish liquid surges every which way, searing painful burns into the skin. Just like that, still drenched, we're shoved into the next room. There we must run a gauntlet between two rows of häftlinge, each with a stack of clothing in his arms. The first one hurls at us underpants spun from rough dark blue linen; the second one, a shirt of the same fabric; the third, the striped inmate-issue trousers we already know well; and his neighbor, the jacket. All of them throw with such speed that it's all we can do to catch everything. The fourth presses round caps onto our heads, and the next one literally whacks us on the head with mismatched crude wooden shoes. By the door they fling the belts at us, and then, like that, we're outside, at the far end of the barrack.

Slave making on a conveyor belt: shove a human being in at one end, and on the other out comes—a häftling.

5

THEY DRIVE US ON RELENTLESSLY. SHIVERING, I THROW
the rags onto my still-dripping-wet body. An hour earlier
I was in good work boots, breeches, and a sheepskin coat, and
now I am excruciatingly cold. It's chilly outside, and the linen
flaps about as the wind catches it from all sides. My wooden
shoes, heavy as lead, clatter frighteningly as I drag my feet like a
convict. I'd become a prisoner in minutes.

By now we are in stripes, like the others, which is how we
march onward. With contorted smiles and looks of dumb be-
wilderment we eye each other's costumes. After ten minutes
of marching down zigzagging roads between the multistory
wooden barracks, we stop before one of them. On the electric
pole in front of us there is a sign: Block XVI.

In one of the windows is an aging woman with thickly colored straw-yellow hair, leaning on her elbow. This barrack houses
women—the only women residents in this city of men. Here
lives a whole contingent of the undoubtedly most abject pros-
titutes of all time: the whores of Auschwitz. This is a brothel.

Nazi thoroughness once again, of course. The women are from
the most varied ethnicities, and naturally they are here not for the
pleasure of ordinary Jewish häftlinge but are at the disposal of

SS soldiers, and perhaps even veteran slave drivers among those Aryans of dubious origin who'd won civil rights in the camp. The same goes for the cinemas, of which more than a few serve to entertain the chosen here, in the capital of the Nation of Death.

The woman with the straw-yellow hair casts a serious, curious stare at the neophytes. Suddenly she vanishes from the window. Moments later she sets her elbows down there yet again, but now she is holding a lit cigarette. She takes a few puffs, and then, accompanied by a telling glance, she drops it slowly, carefully. Right in front of me.

A cigarette. Again, a cigarette. Humanity's message in this improbable world.

Our glances meet. I pick up the burning stick of tobacco, and—not even I know why—call up to her in Hungarian:

"Köszönöm [Thank you]."

It seemed as if she understood me.

People are carrying baskets from the corner. Food. Our first mouthfuls in Auschwitz. My senses still treasure the aroma of the bread we had back in Bačka; I am revolted by the sight of the powder-gray, mud-heavy dollop now before me, the coveted manna of the German cities of death, the tasteless dark, bran-congested bread. We get two days' worth of food, so they told us. The French fellow was right: they were putting us right back into boxcars. We'll be traveling on. They also hand each of us fifteen to twenty decagrams of horse sausage and a double portion of margarine, maybe five decagrams. I smell the sausage, but since it stinks, I cast it aside. Sinful folly. As for the margarine, I have nowhere to put that—it smears in my hand—so in the end I throw that away as well.

Marching yet again. Since arrival we haven't had even a minute of rest. The wooden shoes are heavy and excruciatingly uncomfortable, like handcuffs. The ceaseless distress and the physical and psychological exhaustion drape a fog before my eyes. This first day at Auschwitz is fading into a cool evening, and we're still perpetually on the go. I try figuring out the reason for the harried rush. Is this metropolis of barracks too crowded by now? Is there no room for us even for a night? Or is there an urgent need elsewhere for fresh beasts of burden?

We cut through endless rows of wooden buildings built into streets—streets abuzz with traffic. People in prison uniforms wearing wooden shoes, with tiny triangles in various colors on their jackets. Under each triangle is a stolen personality; in place of their stolen names, everyone there has been baptized with a häftling number. The color of the triangle represents the prisoner's nationality. Many of these people, forced laborers from Eastern Europe, are in civilian rags ornamented with splattered paint, with the word *Ost*—East—on their chests or backs. Even political internees and common criminals of German nationality, as well as homosexuals, have their own ostentatious colors. Auschwitz has become one of their main collection points, too.

At the bottom of the ladder of hell are, naturally, the yellow-starred Jews. They are the greatest in number, and they comprise most of the camp proletariat. Non-Jews of German, Polish, French, Dutch, Greek, and other nationalities landed here in the capital before the Jews, especially those from outside of Poland, so the camp aristocracy developed in the order of their arrival.

Birkenau's chimneys spew that filthy brown smoke ceaselessly above this nightmarish camp of pariahs. Breaks in operations are unknown in this crematorium city. The toxic gas has been belching out day and night for years. The furnaces, fired up until they're glowing white, are trembling; mountains of burning flesh send sooty sparks into the air. There is no escaping the spectacle, which must be watched all day long. Hardly a thing can be seen anymore, thank goodness, for the blessed newcomer, night, tucks away the sinister contours of the row of chimneys under its blanket of darkness.

We flounder along in a long, disorderly line over bumpy farm fields beside the railway embankment. Our guards are closely surrounding us, and the searchlights of the watchtowers are blinding. Far away, on the embankment, a long train emerges from the darkness.

Within minutes we're crammed inside. Once again there are sixty of us in a boxcar. A thin layer of damp wood shavings blankets the floor. There's only room enough for us to curl up beside each other. This time they don't lock the car, but two submachine gun–toting guards hop aboard. The more naïve among us try engaging them in conversation.

"Maul halten [Shut up]*!"*

In the middle of the car is a filthy wooden crate. The privy. So foul that one retches.

It's pitch black inside and out, but the gray ones' handlamps are flickering. We start off, the doors still open.

This journey is just as trying as the first. Trembling in thin rags, I stare greedily at the red-hot end of the cigarette dancing in the hand of one of the guards. Hunger is knocking, too. I take a bite of the bread I've been desperately clutching until now. It tastes good.

Curling up beside each other, we try but fail to sleep. Hauser is crouching beside me. He, too, takes out his bread; he has his margarine ration with him as well.

This surreal nighttime journey seems unbearable. After Auschwitz and Birkenau, without a name, without a self, not knowing from where or to where. Even worse than the first journey. The submachine gun–toting guards are looming by the open doors. Slip past them and step out into the dark? A passing thought, but as enticing as opium: momentary floating, and then, everything is over. Hauser is thinking the same thing. He whispers:

"We should jump out. Let's try."

"Madness," I reply. "Do you want to escape or be butchered? Escape in this ridiculous, attention-getting garb is impossible anyway."

"Who's talking about escape? To die, to die . . ."

He's crying. While mechanically munching away.

"You'll always have time to die," I say, but my voice isn't convincing even for me.

"Say, is this sort of thing possible to survive?" he asks.

"No."

"And then?"

"It's not, but it must be."

Hauser falls silent. Finally, exhaustion takes hold of me, too, and I fall into a restless half sleep. Every minute I'm roused by people tumbling over me. That makeshift privy in the middle of the car is always occupied. The bran bread and the soup made of horsemeat sausages gone bad causes diarrhea. At times I'm in a daze; it would be good to fall asleep completely. But that's impossible. The sharp nighttime cold is biting at my chest.

How long will this journey last? Two hours? Five? Dawn filters in through the open doors. The flatlands remain behind us; we're now rumbling on between forest-cloaked mountainsides. Alert and motionless, the guards are watching us. They haven't slept, either: they've been smoking cigarettes and pipes, and muttering with each other all night long. Now they too dig out some food. The same sort of bread as ours emerges from their bags. Carefully they spread a thin layer of margarine, meanwhile gulping from their canteens.

A labyrinth of power lines whizzes by us. Where are we, and what time could it be? It's been a good while since we left Auschwitz, but the train is chugging along quite slowly. We can see little of the surrounding countryside, and approaching the door is strictly prohibited. Once again, that tiny window with the bars is our only view, as it was yesterday—a year ago, one hundred years ago—going to Auschwitz from home.

The journey seems to take an eternity. It doesn't matter; anywhere will do, in any circumstances, if only we'd finally arrive somewhere, so I could stretch out somewhere, lose myself somehow, like ridding myself of some loathsome disease.

We suddenly rumble above rail switches, like so often before, and the train slows down. We've arrived. We've arrived somewhere.

Indeed. The train heaves as it grinds to a halt, and our machine gunners jump off. We stomp over to the door, drinking in the outside world. We're by a tiny, one-story station or, rather, guardhouse: Mühlhausen.

Behind it, in front of it, and all around it is a dense forest cloaked in dark green, with mounds of glittering coal beside the three parallel tracks. It is unusual and beautiful. The sun shines upon the myriad granules of coal from behind a curtain of foliage. Here, too, there is a fabric of electric power lines.

The small mountain station is completely deserted. A few rusty trucks on one of the tracks seem to have been forgotten there years ago.

"Lower Silesia," spreads the word. "A region of quarries and coal mines."

We head off in groups of five to a nearby clearing. We stand in a square formation on lush grass, mud clumped all over our wooden shoes. They're waiting for us. In front of two desks in one corner of the clearing are SS officers. Lots of other officers all around. They're unabashedly sizing us up, like traders at a livestock market. They're gesticulating, pointing toward us.

A brief procedure ensues. We need to pass by the two desks. At one, a cardboard tag is attached to a length of rough cord hung around our necks, and at the other we need to read out the number on the cardboard.

33031. That's my number. Starting now, I'm no longer me, but 33031. Much more a number than, say, an inmate with a life sentence, whose identity and possessions are kept in a prison office.

I was never one for numbers. I didn't believe in their magic. My measure of value has always been words. My capacity to remember numbers is so weak that I've forgotten my own phone number at times. And yet, now, the sole distinguishing mark of my future existence is etched into me within moments. The family and given names among the voluminous data on my birth certificate, and the nicknames by which my mother and my sweetheart once called me, disappear. *Dreiunddreissignulleinunddreissig*—33031—is what I'm called from now on. In this alone, and in nothing else, am I different from 74516 or 125993.

The next station is an empty barn. An abandoned workshop of sorts. There's a desk here, too, with officers. They have us cast off our rags. We step naked up onto a crate with a big, flat surface that is serving as a podium. We turn around like models. At the desk an SS doctor is ranking us. Yet again, this is it for the medical exam. Not once going forward do we notice any consequence or even a trace of this ranking.

After this recruitment, exhausted, we hurriedly throw our clothes back on. Back to the clearing. It's well past noon, and since yesterday morning all I've had to eat was a little bit of bran bread. I'm tormented by hunger, staggering from weakness. Never will I understand how, after all this, I endured the twenty-kilometer forced uphill march that came next.

We started off at short intervals, divided into groups of two hundred. Which contingent I would be swept into, and which death camp I'd eventually be part and parcel of, was purely a matter of chance.

Well-maintained mountain roads and scattered clusters of houses signal villages. A few larger buildings somewhat far apart from each other, one or two factories or mines—that's all these communities comprise, but not one is without a bank, an inn, and the local Nazi Party headquarters strewn with flags and decorated with potted plants.

Our new Mühlhausen guards are no longer submachine gun–toting young SS men. Prodding on the listless, teetering, miserable marchers are older-looking, Wehrmacht territorial army soldiers in worn, dull-green uniforms. No rest: the Germans aren't tired. We're even more so. With every step the wooden shoes cause my wounded feet to bleed, the rough, raw leather at the top of the shoe plunging like a knife into my burning ankles.

"*Los!* . . . *Los!* . . . *Bewegung!* . . . [Come on! . . . Come on! . . . Move!]"

There's a burst of prodding at almost every step. From the

end of our contingent comes an animal-like whimpering. The voice shouts, then wails. Someone who stopped to pull off his work boots, sticky with blood, is being brought to his senses with a rifle butt. All of us are out of energy. Even now it seems that this miserable journey will never end.

We pass by a couple of camps, too, on each side of the road that stretches between the villages. They all look hauntingly the same. The green-painted round tents, the watchtower with the machine-pistol-toting guard, the sentries' barracks beyond the barbed wire, tremulously slow-moving häftlinge, a pipe-smoking German guard, and above it all, the Silesian sky, which is always rocking clouds to and fro—the same thing everywhere, despairingly so.

The road turns up a thickly wooded slope. People in blue-striped uniforms are moving about on a hilltop, some thirty or forty meters above us. They're like us. Using pickaxes and spades, they're cutting a yellow strip of clay into the hillside. They throw the heavy clumps of muddy earth from ditches up into "Japans," or iron boxcars, shaped like dough-kneading troughs. Other häftlinge are standing up against the boxcars and rolling them along. They're carrying iron rods and using them to push rocks out of the way. To the left, on another hilltop, are the familiar green tents. Even higher up is a wooden watchtower, with a sentry and a machine gun. The iron boxcars screech in protest, and somewhere an invisible cement mixer is pounding away. We hear drawn-out shouts:

"*Los! . . . Bewegung! . . . Los!*"

It seems we have arrived.

6

THE MUNICIPALITY WHOSE TERRITORY THIS CAMP IS ON IS called Eule. It's considered one of the most picturesque spots in Lower Silesia. Nearby, despite this being a mining region, there are several sanatoriums high up in the mountains. At one time, those with heart trouble took refuge here from the summer heat. It's always on the cool side for the season, and ever-wandering cloud caravans filter the intensity of the sun. If you're dressed for the weather and have a name, money, cigarettes, and newspapers, being a guest at a spa around here wouldn't be so bad.

We learned all this from the older residents of the camp, which is still under construction; we're the third shipment to arrive. We find hardly a few hundred people here. Ninety percent of them are Greek; the rest are Dutch, French, and Polish. There are also a few from Budapest. All Jews, naturally.

The camp's nascent hierarchy has developed in line with the distribution of nationalities. The Lagerälteste is a short, cocky French Jew. He has a name, too. He's called Max, and word around here has it that he had a nightclub in Paris with an impeccably bad reputation. He is the all-powerful lord of the camp. A malicious, merciless, mercurial lord. His swishing cane is just as fearsome as the whip and the revolver of the SS sergeant who is the camp commandant.

Michel, the clerk, is from Amsterdam. The work is carried out by three companies. The Waldenburg branch of Georg Urban Civil and Structural Engineering AG leases most of the digging work; Kemna AG drills tunnels; and Baugesellschaft builds the structures in what is planned to be a sprawling city of barracks. The entire aristocracy of häftlinge comprises three company kapos with the deputy kapos, and, yes, a few Blockältesten, or block commanders. Naturally, aside from the Lagerälteste—the supreme kapo—and the clerk. There is no kitchen, and so there is no kitchen aristocracy. High-ranking "medics" are likewise absent for now. Soup is brought in insulated cauldrons, in trucks, from an unknown location.

Our arrival does not cause much of a stir. The hillside laborers cast us passing glances, dull indifference in their eyes. The thin Lagerälteste receives the list accompanying us from the head guard. He reads out the numbers. The tents await us on the hilltop, empty and drafty. This is the first time I've seen such facilities up close. The tents are round and made of papier-mâché-like plastic. Inside each, a wood-plank floor runs along the wall all around a circus ring–like layer of earth divided into twenty-four sharp-edged triangles of the same size. Each triangle is big enough so a scrawny person might be able to stretch out inside it. Even so, the "residents" are necessarily packed in like sardines, for we're herded in groups of thirty into the tents. A restful repose is out of the question.

We carry in the wood shavings. They serve as our lairs. In death camps, wood shavings stand in for straw. Never have I seen straw around here. In this land of unproductive, clay-clogged, saline soil, straw is held in high regard as fodder for livestock. We get two bales of wood shavings per tent, just enough to sprinkle over the damp plank floor. Thin, synthetic blankets wind up on the wretched berths, and already that dreadful word rings out, for the first time, that word that later chased our agitated hearts up into our throats:

"*Appell* [Roll call]*!*"

The Appell is an assembly, an issuing of commands, a reading out of the duty roster, an occasion for reporting, a cross-examination, a trial, and a carrying out of sentences all wrapped up into a single concept and a single act. The Appell usually takes place at daybreak, before we head off to work, and in the evening, on getting back. Usually. But that rusty iron rod hanging from a tree—the camp gong—rings out practically every day until lights-out, even during the rest hours we have at our disposal. It signals an emergency Appell. We can never know how many hours we'll be stuck there, tormented practically to death, in wind, in rain, at taut attention; and, moreover, we can never know when we'll be witness to, and perhaps the victims of, a death sentence pronounced and carried out.

Unsuspectingly, we assemble for the first Appell. We form a large square in front of the tents. Those who came here previously line up in separate columns by the companies they work for. On the edge is the little group of camp cleaners. In the middle of the human square are the Lagerälteste and the clerk. The company kapos are scrambling pompously about in front of their columns, straightening the lines with blows from their cudgels. Weary almost to the point of unconsciousness, half-starved, the people keep looking with numb terror toward the middle of the square. The Lagerälteste screams at the top of his lungs:

"*Achtung* [Attention]*!*"

The mass of people stiffens in taut attention. With regulation motions the round prisoners' caps come flying off the shaved heads.

An SS sergeant. He must be around forty or fifty. Every night, after the Appell, he takes out his violin and, hesitatingly, plays raspy, maudlin tunes for the listening stars. So far he's beaten twenty-two people to death with his cane and shot nine to death with his revolver during the Appells, for all those lined up to see. He's a hefty Teuton with watery blue eyes, blond hair, and glasses. He has a slaughterhouse in some small town in Pomerania. His wife is now running the business. Yes, there's a war on; duty calls. . . .

A revolver swells from his waist, and a whip is lurking under the belt. He now steps to the middle of our formation and, with a wave, summons the clerk and the Lagerälteste, who is holding the roster. With those henchmen in his wake, he struts right up to the rows. As the Lagerälteste now reads out the names five at a time, the SS sergeant snaps his whip effortlessly on the shoulders of the first person in each group.

This time the tally is in order. God forbid it be otherwise. The inquisition is next. The Lagerälteste glances at the sheet of paper in his hand, and shouts:

"21825!"

Someone emerges from a row and shuffles toward the middle, resignation in his listless steps. He knows what awaits him, for cross-examination usually follows a complaint lodged by a civilian observer or an SS guard.

"Stinking Jew, from ten to twelve thirty you played hooky from work. Where were you? What do you imagine? That we're filling you up with free food?"

We don't hear the reply, only the swishing of the whip. This is warming up.

21825 has to stand on all fours. This is just a formality, actually, pure tradition, since most of the blows land on the head.

"Fifty," snaps the violinist.

The Lagerälteste carries out the sentence. The Pomeranian butcher doesn't bother with details but supervises conscientiously, and the Lagerälteste puts his all into the blows—even more so because if the camp god suspects shenanigans it often happens that the blows continue on the head of the one meting out the sentence.

After the third blow 21825 is wallowing full-length on the ground. At first he lets out unfettered, beastly screams, but by the twentieth blow the harrowing sound has subsided into whimpering. The twenty-first, twenty-second, and fiftieth shower down on a motionless mass. The Lagerälteste waves a hand, and three people step from the group of cleaners and drag away the victim.

"27111!" the call resounds again in the tremulous silence.

The next one steps forward. Again, the blows come showering down. The scene in Imre Madách's nineteenth-century Hungarian play *The Tragedy of Man* that is set in a commune in the future comes vaguely to mind. The same thing, and what a big difference. The old man in the play metes out but minor punishment; but here the spectacled man from Pomerania is committing murder. Madách had only been dreaming; Hitler is realizing.

The whip cracks on the bodies of three more victims, and then the Appell is over.

I'm staggering from dizziness. I'm nauseous. Standing in line for our daily rations: bread, with a spoonful of slightly sour jam. We newcomers don't yet get soup; the kitchen has yet to be notified of us. I gobble down the bread in a few bites, and then the hunger is even more excruciating. Two things are unheard of in a death camp: smiles and satiety.

Eight thirty at night. A half hour before lights-out. We chat listlessly in front of the tents. Among the few Budapesters here is the son of János Vázsonyi, Hungary's onetime Jewish minister of justice, who, with little success but headstrong ambition, once tried his own hand at everyday politics. One time, I vaguely recall, we introduced ourselves at some dinner party.

He's lost half his weight, and that perpetual smooth smile of his has stiffened into a painful grimace on his sunken face. He is visibly dying, though he's been here only a few weeks. They say he's attempted suicide three times so far. He's a passionate smoker, and the nicotine withdrawal is especially hard on him. With delirious yearning he fantasizes about mounds of cigarettes, heaps of tobacco. He's like a human again only on those rare occasions when he manages to access a cigarette butt or a few specks of tobacco. At such times he gathers the Hungarians around him and embarks on long disquisitions that invariably close on an optimistic note:

"They can't take more than another couple weeks. No, no way. The moment the invasion comes, a rapid collapse will be awaiting them. Liberation is approaching, you'll see; we'll go home."

He's saying this sort of thing even now. Smoldering away in his wasted, trembling hand is the stub of a run-of-the-mill

Caporal cigarette. He got the barely smoked cigarette today from an English POW at the station, where he'd been working in a group loading boxcars. At length, with lively gestures, he tells the tale of his luck. He is happy.

By now we newcomers are puttering about in the tents, readying our pallets. Those from Sombor, Subotica, and Novi Sad are trying to get into the same tent. The Lagerälteste and the clerk show up, too. They collegially ask about news from the front. The clerk then strikes the gong, which lets out its raspy peal, and already the motionless night settles over us slaves.

7

F OUR AM. THEY KICK THE SIDE OF THE TENT.
    "*Auf* [Up]!"
The wake-up crew is running along the row of tents. The clerk is furiously clanging the iron rod hanging from the tree. The half-conscious slaves jump up. Those who took their striped rags off at night now hastily throw them back on. Washing up is hardly an option. Hundreds charge at the small number of dripping faucets in the yard, but only a few people manage to wet their hands and faces in the ice-cold water. Drinking water is strictly prohibited, since it's infected. Without exception this is the case in all camps.

A new peal from the gong signals the prelude to the early-morning Appell. We've got to hurry, since those who aren't standing in line within seconds are playing with their lives. To miss roll call is one of the most grievous offenses: the punishment is often death.

It's hard to imagine something more hopeless and dispiriting than this sort of early-morning disturbance amid the dire circumstances that are already a given. The certainty that yet another long day full of torment and dangers will ensue, that hunger and whipping, filth and lice, await, fills a person at every turn with the agonizing desire to die. *To end it all*—so comes this refrain yet again in the listless consciousness. And these were just spring mornings. Later, amid the despair of even bleaker moments at daybreak in November and December, a häftling will recall what's happening now as jovial dawn exercises. At the moment there was hope, after all, that the sun would shine for a few minutes or hours and soak through our frost-encrusted linen clothes.

But who was now thinking of November mornings? This was already more than enough. Busy as we were drowning in the miseries of the present, we could not imagine that even greater horrors could follow.

There is no breakfast. Only the higher-ups' voices can be heard as the company kapos are hustling their charges into lines as the men are drowning in hacking coughs. I awake even more exhausted than when I lay down. The hard bed, sprinkled with wood shavings, does not ensure rest, and my empty stomach steals my dreams.

Dung collects in stinking puddles around the frighteningly squalid, squatting privy. Those relieving themselves soil each other in the pitch-black darkness. Shadows squelch about in the abominable pond, cursing, pushing and shoving, sighing. Cigarette stubs are glowing in one or two hands. Others, watching those tiny embers burn away, beg and haggle for a drag. The smokers squat possessively above the dung, moaning away, taking deep, greedy drags. In the Land of Auschwitz, the first thing to wither away is the instinct of disgust. The more frugal among us, who still have a piece of bread from yesterday, sell a morsel for a drag. Hasty trades are made: those who've given up their bread thirstily swallow the smoke, while those who've parted with cigarette stubs chew away on chunks of bread while squatting.

The Lagerälteste cries out:

"*Antreten* [Line up]!"

A mad rush ensues. We line up unbelievably fast in the early-morning cold. We newcomers stand in a separate row. Civilians are accompanying the camp commandant: these are the foremen of the slave-holding companies. The selection of the fresh arrivals ensues. It is hauntingly like a slave market.

Each company lays claim to a certain number of slave laborers. On the one hand, each tries to get itself the strongest ones; on the other hand, the German speakers. Kemna is the most dreaded of the three companies. Not only on account of its vicious civilian slave drivers, whose acts of cruelty we'd heard hair-raising stories about yesterday, but also because this is the company that drills tunnels here. In our situation, tunnel work is the worst of the worst. For now, Urban AG is focusing on aboveground work: digging, rock crushing, the laying down of industrial sidetracks, but even with them, it would all lead to tunnel work. Those who got here earlier say that Baugesellschaft, the barracks construction firm, is the best—among other reasons, because its work site is the camp itself, so the daily labor is not made worse by an agonizing walk of several kilometers to a site far afield and back again to the camp. Naturally, those who arrived earlier also vied for Baugesellschaft. So we started off here at quite a disadvantage; the newcomers were needed by Kemna and Urban. I managed to avoid Kemna, so from there on in I was among the slaves at Georg Urban AG. For my labor the company pays Hitler's state two marks a day to cover my "board" and my "apparel," and I harbor no illusions that I won't have to earn this sum with blood.

The Urban AG slaves line up separately, and the junior kapos select their groups. Today fresh divisions are forming for new work sites. I get swept up in one at random. The groups of twenty to twenty-five are dispersed in every direction, each accompanied by an SS guard and a civilian foreman.

I'm in luck: my work site isn't far. I'll be hauling industrial train-track rails. We stand at the square formed by crossed iron rails and lift at the kapo's "Heave, ho!" and then carry. It's unusually hard. The meters stretch out endlessly; meanwhile the Greeks, with whom I'm trudging in one yoke, are slacking off. I'm struck that through some clever maneuvering they've ensured that a weight meant to be carried by two is bearing down on me. My arms feel as if they'll rip right off my torso each and every moment as I carry on, flushed, dizzy, eyes dimming.

This is my initiation in Eule.

8

F OURTEEN DAYS OF CROSS-BEARING AGONY PASS. THAT
bygone life, the world beyond the barbed wire, is a beautiful dream, one I had once upon a time, long ago indeed. Perhaps not even in this life. I reach for my face but can see even
without a mirror how long it is. Staggering, I throw myself at
the brownish-black bunker soup like a wild beast along with
the others. Constant hunger exacerbates my sense of furious,
helpless yearning after a smoke. As long as it's available, I keep
buying tobacco from the Greeks in exchange for the daily ration
of bread.

The Greeks are the camp's peddlers. They are amazingly
clever at scalping, they are hypocrites, and they are crafty. They
get their hands on everything, and they demand exorbitant
prices for everything. They are mostly eastern Jews deported
here from Ioannina and Patras and the Greek islands. They are
swarthy, wild, inhuman, and full of peculiar, alien instincts we
don't understand, can't understand, and have cast off perhaps
centuries ago. I stare at them with shocked incredulity, at these
living refutations of Jewish world solidarity, of distinctive racial
characteristics, and of all the Nazi nonsense trumpeted about
the international uniformity of the Jewish soul.

There's hardly an educated one among them. The vast majority are staggeringly ignorant. As for their occupations, most are traveling salesmen and huckstering merchants. Their perpetual oafish grins are nerve-racking. They know a lot that we don't. With spectacular skill they ingratiate themselves with the Germans in a matter of days. The Greeks have an extraordinary ability to make shiftlessness seem like feverish effort, hard work. They are so skilled at this that even the vigilant, suspicious Germans fall for it. These Greeks are idlers by nature, they're lazy, and they're quick to slack off, and yet it's them our guards and the Meister—the civilian foreman—have stand before us as examples. The Greeks are the ones who bum cigar stubs out of the mouths of the German slave drivers. Each of us keeps an eye on those stubs furtively, anxiously, awaiting the big moment when they burn down to the lips of the slave drivers, who then flick them away. But the Greeks always get to them first.

The Greeks can't even learn the simplest German expressions, but they are constantly lolling about and sucking up to the Meister, fussing about, denouncing. Lacking language skills, they do all this with gesticulations, flailing arms and legs.

"Ungar nix ahhrbeit, grek gut ahhrbeiten gut!" They jabber this broken German rendition of "Hungarians don't work; Greeks work well" ten or twenty times a day into the credulous ear of the Meister, the German. So the Greek always gets the recognition and the cigarette.

Their artistry in thievery is unrivaled. Stealing—especially stealing bread, which means life—is a capital offense. Usually it's the prisoners themselves who take revenge straightaway and without mercy. Often the bloodthirsty crowd surges forward and lynches a bread thief caught red-handed. This sort of dastardly act—stealing bread—incites public passion in an instant, heightening our awareness that today or tomorrow someone might pilfer the treasure any one of us has hidden in a rag or a sack of cement.

Ten months later, in the Dörnhau death camp, I witnessed several instances of such justice being meted out. Before my very eyes, not a few people in the final stages of dying of hunger who'd been caught stealing bread were pulled, pushed, torn, and kicked to death.

Catching our Greek "comrades" in the act was hard. To this day I don't understand their shrewd methods and tricks. Never will I comprehend how they managed to lift out the bread I'd hidden deep inside the course sack of straw that, moreover, I'd taken care to slip under my head. Not a trace of a cut was visible on the burlap, so they had to reach deep under the side of a sheet and feel about under my head with utter care to avoid rousing me from my uneasy half sleep. And this required composure worthy of wonder and no less remarkable sleight of hand. Indeed, the Greek häftlinge were wonder workers.

Fourteen days in Eule . . .

With treacherous speed I sink into the muck of the camp. Squealing and flailing away, I struggle to get my hands on a lighter pickax, for easier work lugging rails, for thicker soup, for even a tiny spot to sleep. Screaming inarticulately, I wallow about with the others, struggling to get at a carrot in the mud by the road; gnashing my teeth, I jump at every cigarette stub on the ground.

Wake-up is at 4:00 AM, and by 5:00 we're at work, which lasts until 6:00 PM, with a noon half-hour break. The chaos of calls to assemble, of evening Appells, and of food distribution robs us of another hour and a half. Around 7:30 you can think of yourself a bit, too. The faucets are trickling just enough to wet your face and hands, which are thickly coated with earth, dust, cement, grime. Also, you can have your wounds bandaged, assuming you're able to find the surly, clueless Pole playing doctor here, though back home—in the best-case scenario—he was a nurse. Then again, he might have been a rag peddler or a boilermaker.

I'm on my feet seventeen hours a day, at least fourteen of those in backbreaking work. The liter of cold fluid called soup that they ladle out into a rusty can serving as a mess tin doesn't relieve my tormenting hunger. Greedily, practically without chewing, I swallow down my quarter loaf of bread. It is probably forty decagrams, but it's heavy, tasteless, unnourishing. Unfilling. I feel sorry for the frugal, the careful, among us. Measuring to the centimeter, they cut their bread into paper-thin slices. When the opportunity arises to buy cigarettes, naturally most of my share winds up in the bellies of the Greeks.

There's *Zulage*—extra pay—as well. Fifteen to twenty grams of margarine, jam, or a thin slice of horse salami that most often already stinks. Once a week we get the star of soups: milk soup with the top skimmed off. Sweet, warm, soothing. Strips of pasta are swimming around inside. At such times our taste buds are exulting over the rare sensation of flavor. We swear to order milk soup every day if we get home. We'll hold milk soup orgies; we'll wallow in milk soup.

Yet another holiday feast: potatoes floating in sauce. Five or six stunted bits of unpeeled boiled potatoes in a couple tablespoons of sauce. Infrequent though it is, this food makes up for it with its density. Other than the Zulage and bread, it is the only nourishment we get that's not in liquid form. Both this and the milk soup are rare delicacies.

The menu nearly always comprises carrot soup, sorrel soup, or so-called bunker soup. Each portion—soup, bread, Zulage—has precisely enough calories, just enough nutrients, absolutely necessary to maintain life. To maintain it, not to protect it. The latter isn't important at all. They calculate the häftling's capacity to work and his lifespan as a matter of months. When he drops dead, the securely locked trains will spew out more well-fattened, fresh goods. Calorie calculations at death camps are the work of diligent and untalented German scientists, the product of me-thodical German experimentation and absurdly detailed digging and delving. To eat until you're full—that's different. There's no need for that.

Those German specialists are the ones who invented bunker soup, that musty-flavored liquidy pulp; powder cheese; molasses jam with its horrible stench; and other häftling delicacies.

It's pitch-black outside at 8:00 PM, and an oil lamp is flick-ering in the middle of the tent. Dead-tired people are stretch-ing out on the tent's triangles. We're expelling the warm liquid in disgusting belches; we're dressing our boils. We're scratching ourselves.

I'm in a tent with those from Novi Sad. For days now I've been working with my old friend Béla Maurer, the lawyer and newspaper reporter who used to be an editor at one of the Hungarian-language dailies in Yugoslavia. I haven't seen him in a while, ever since we were in Topola. There he was wrong indeed in doubting that we'd be deported. He lets me squeeze in beside him in the tent. Aside from me and little Bolgár, everyone here is from Novi Sad.

Maurer is a kind, clever person; everyone likes him. He arrived a hefty 120 kilos, and, as a veteran of indigestion, he dreaded every mouthful that wasn't dietetic. For weeks he didn't touch food, instead digesting his rolls of fat, living on them. By now he too has adapted. He can't be more than 70 kilos; he spoons down the bunker soup like any one of us. His belly—so he claims—no longer hurts.

Thirsty, we listen to his delusional explications:

"You've got to do like me. Simply assess the situation. What's the situation? The situation is that one must endure four months of this."

"Easy for you to say," says the scrawny, ever-sad Gleiwitz. "You brought a pot of fat with you."

"Nonsense. You can get through this just the same. There's not a person of average health who doesn't have reserves enough in them to survive four months. And it's a mathematical certainty that in four months this will be over. When we left, everyone with good sense knew that the Germans had already lost when their blitzkrieg on the Eastern Front failed."

Imhof, a lawyer, quietly objects.

"That's right; they lost. And we, with them."

Maurer, temperamental as he is, flies off the handle.

"We're going home! Do you understand? Home. The Anglo-Saxons may have even made their landing by now. After the invasion, events will unfold rapidly, one after another. No more uneventfulness. To the east, the Soviets have the initiative, and the little satellite states are wavering. What can Hitler be hoping for?"

"Nothing," replied Imhof, doubling down: "Just like us."

"Nonsense! The collapse isn't far off. Four months at most."

Everyone in the tent is listening with bated breath. Hope spreads its wings. We're capable of believing again, up until the Appell at dawn the next day. The forceful, persuasive Maurer has seeded confidence all around. I alone demur.

"Just look around you, Béla! Take a load of this material plenty; of all the first-rate lumber, iron, steel, and cement that arrives here every day, of all these strong young men the front can do without in the fifth year of the war! Where's the scarcity? Where's the shadow of a coming collapse?"

"Where?" Béla responds. "I'll tell you where. First, in the bellies ... Second, in the souls. Yesterday I had a one-on-one conversation with Jozef. You know, the short blond guy. The Meister at the quarry. I've gotten to know him really well. A true German. Herd mentality. He has a psychological need for obedience to superiors, cruelty to underlings. But I convinced him that I'm a judge, and he was in awe. He named me junior kapo with his team. Well, this Jozef admitted to me that as a manual laborer he gets two eggs a month. Beyond that, among other things, every day he gets just twenty-five decagrams of bran bread and two—yes, two—cigarettes. Or a comparable amount of pipe tobacco. Jozef is a die-hard smoker, and since he can't afford the black-market price of cigarettes, one and a half marks, he smokes strawberry leaves."

"Serves him right," I cut in. "Yesterday I was drying horse dung."

"I'll write about this someday," says Maurer malevolently, with the superior air of nonsmokers. "When I go home, I'll write the novel of Auschwitz. It will be six hundred pages.

"So our Jozef has resorted to strawberry leaves," he continues. "Today he is still a committed Nazi, but who knows what tomorrow will bring. Dictators are not supposed to get beaten up, and they sure shouldn't go joking around with the bellies of their underlings. This Jozef is still Hitler's man. The crazy doctrines, the murky slogans, still live within him, but you can't shout 'Heil Hitler!' for long on twenty-five decagrams of bread. And maybe it occurs to Jozef that his wife and kid back in Saxony get only fifteen decagrams. They've got nails, boards, cement, and steel. So it seems. But bellies can't be filled with nails. You can see with your own eyes that not even the SS soldiers eat much better food."

He doesn't convince me.

"They get separate soup," I retort. "With meat. They get more bread; they get coffee; they get cigarettes. Clothes, shoes, money. They don't work fourteen hours a day. Enough already, Béla! We're facing eighty million murderers, and if the noose is tightened, they'll do us in first."

Gleiwitz dryly adds:

"And this is only third-class service behind the front. Rest assured that soldiers on the front lines get chocolate, too. Tobacco? As much as fits in them. Which is not to mention what they can pillage."

"There aren't eighty million murderers," says Maurer, flinging his arms about as usual. "At most . . ."

"At most ten million," said Gleiwitz, completing the thought. "But there definitely are that many, damn them. . . ."

Those listening receive these words with bitter joviality. For his part, Maurer doesn't give in, far from it. The people can't be compared to a bloodthirsty, demented clique, he insists.

Meanwhile my thoughts run like this:

That's right. You can't pronounce one big nation that has played a decisive role in every aspect of history as far as anyone can remember—a people who have given the world Goethe and Beethoven, as well as the Nobel Prize–winning scientific minds Robert Koch and Wilhelm Röntgen—guilty of the collective sin of being maniacal murderers on the one hand, thieving murderers on the other. Such thinking is an affront not only to the analytical mind but also to human instinct. And yet it is a fact that of the eighty million strong mass of this "thinking people," at least ten million have a direct or indirect interest and even employment in the machinery of a great outrage against humanity. Consciously or not, millions here are accomplices to a crime. Why then does it occur to so few of them that they are committing a crime? Terror insufficiently explains the almost total absence of resistance. Perhaps one really can't talk of eighty million murderers, but of a few million one can. By all means one can.

This is a singular people. A bunch of inner contradictions, a bunch of dumbfounding extremes, a singular people that has given the world not only Robert Koch but also Ilse Koch, the Witch of Buchenwald, the most perverse woman serial killer of all time, not only Kepler but also Himmler. Both those obsessed with understanding and the gravediggers of civilization. Humanists and sadist killers by turns. Napoleon's soldiers carried marshal's batons in their haversacks; Hitler's philistines, castrating knives.

But I don't say a thing. A May evening breeze steals into the tent through the glassless little window, flickering the flame of the oil lamp. There are thirty of us here, and it's almost curfew time. We're waiting for little Bolgár, who'd been a technical university student back in Hungary, in Szeged, and who now works in the Todt people's planning barrack. He had a fabulous stroke of luck, and his situation is singular indeed. He inhabits an Eldorado of food scraps and cigar stubs; he works at a table. He draws, and he walks behind engineers carrying measuring instruments.

"Not even he will be killed by his good heart," Maurer says

of little Bolgár, since the short, tiny young man—no more than 150 centimeters tall—never shared his treasures with anyone. And yet he has the opportunity to peek into newspapers, and he supplies us with regular servings of credible news gladly, with evident pleasure.

After little Bolgár's arrival we put out the oil lamp, and without even a prelude the boy gets right down to filling us in on the latest. His memory is exceptional: practically word for word he quotes from the Nazi news agency DNB reports in *Schweidnitzer Beobachter*, the local paper.

Then he tells us what he heard from Todt's people. Bolgár always brings some encouraging news. The Allied landing has not yet begun, but rumors of the big event are already in the air. Even the Germans are expecting it any day, discussing among themselves the prospects and possible outcomes.

"Today that fat guy, Gaedicke—you know, the Berlin engineer and father of four I've told you about before—offered me some of his beer. And what do you think he said? 'Well, häftling, soon we'll be going home.' That's what he said. I swear."

"As he imagines it," Gleiwitz's voice crackles in the dark.

"What?"

"That he's going home."

Maurer sits up on his pallet.

"He might not be going, but we are."

"That's right," says Grosz, the millionaire textile merchant.

"And what if, before the surrender, they simply destroy the camps?" asks Gleiwitz. "If they lock us in the barracks and simply light them up? If they send us to the gas chambers? Or mow us down in a heap with machine guns?"

"Unfortunately, that's all too believable," says Grosz, in a fretting, anxious tone. "If they retreat, they won't make a big fuss. It's all the same to them anyway."

The textile merchant is by now speaking through his tears. He's among the frugal here, divvying up his bread ration for breakfast, lunch, and dinner. He watches out for himself, saving his strength. Trembling, he hopes to the core that he will, after all, be able to record this little Auschwitz liability in his business records.

The camp bell rings nine o'clock. Gleiwitz speaks with the full weight of authority vested in his role as *Stubenälteste*—Room Elder.

"Good night, comrades! God save us all. Good night. . . ."

Here these clichéd words come across as mindless sarcasm indeed, one whose mechanical meaning never penetrates its conceptual depths when uttered back home. Is it even possible to have a good night? In such a place?

Stretching out beside me, Maurer touches my shoulder.

"Hey, I think you were right, after all. Do you remember *The Maurizius Case*?"

"Do I remember what?"

"Jakob Wasserman's novel *Der Fall Maurizius*—*The Maurizius Case*."

"Somewhat," I replied. "Why did this occur to you now?"

"All those millions of murderers. You know, that part with Klakusch, the old prison guard with the yellow beard. After hearing Maurizius's story and getting a sense of his whole being, this Klakusch becomes convinced that Maurizius is innocent, that he has been sentenced unjustly, that he has been languishing in prison as an innocent man for eighteen years. How does Klakusch reply to society? He hangs himself."

"And so?" I ask.

"There may be some truth in the notion that we're not facing eighty million murderers, after all, but a few million—yes. I know that lots of Germans maybe even feel sorry for us, but those like Klakusch, who stand up for what they believe in, who take risks, who, at the cost of their own lives, call the most brutal wholesale slaughters of the past thousand years by their names, well, there are no such Klakusches, or there are infinitesimally few. But don't you let on to them here that I too—"

"What do you expect?" I asked. "Surely you don't expect people to stand out in Berlin in the middle of Alexanderplatz and right there on that spot tell Hitler the truth to his face?"

"Not exactly. But something like this: Ten righteous people in Sodom and Gomorrah. For whom I could forgive the others."

"Not just ten. There are ten thousand. You're forgetting that not just Jews are suffering in Auschwitz, but German gentiles, too. Political prisoners. And you can find them not only in Auschwitz. Dachau, Mauthausen, Buchenwald, Bergen-Belsen, and Gross-Rosen are also full of them."

"That's not the real thing," Maurer insists. "Not what I'm thinking of. It wasn't political conviction that led old Klakusch to that noose he'd tied himself. It's both more, and less, than this. Simple, human compassion. This is what's missing from Hitler's Teutonia, and this is why the madness can get so out of control. Millions cannot be forced to accept moral responsibility for such acts if within these millions there isn't some subconscious, implicit assent at work. The Germans are a people of musicians, thinkers—and sadists. Neither the Russian, French, British, Serbian, nor any other nation could have invented the gas-powered automobile or Birkenau's mechanized human slaughterhouses. Only the German. Just like a seal can't give birth to a kangaroo."

Maurer falls silent. I'm thinking, *Well now, we've switched roles. He is now attacking what he was defending minutes ago.*

We're adrift in a sea of moaning human bodies tossing and turning about. Sleep is impossible, and yet a sort of uneasy trance embraces me all the same.

Even such spasmodic conversations are rare. Hardly a night in the camp passes in what feels like human company. A relatively calm day, an Appell that unfolds without any lashing, and a few puffs of tobacco are necessary to so much as get us in the mood to say anything.

The fact that spring doesn't want to take hold makes our thousand miseries even worse. As if this region were also damned, we rarely get even two or three hours of sunlight. The weather forecast is rendered uncertain by the ever-passing clouds. Our camp is flanked by hills to the south, but the north winds roll in freely, tearing furiously at our shantytown.

We're well into June. We arrived six weeks ago, and the camp is rising before our eyes. The soldiers and civilian slave drivers of Baugesellschaft—the construction company—are working valiantly. Soon two large barracks comprising twenty-four rooms each stand ready at the foot of the hill, below our tents. Twenty other similarly huge barracks are being built. They look far more comfortable than our tents. The completed barracks are empty for now. Three-hundred-liter boilers have meanwhile arrived for the kitchens that are yet to be built. There are more sentries, and barracks similar to ours are arising lightning fast beyond the barbed wire for the soldiers and Todt's people. By all indications, we'll be a big camp.

The poor diggers get home every day looking increasingly pale, with swollen, bloodshot eyes. They are boring a colossal tunnel five kilometers from the camp. This tunnel is rapidly wolfing down what's left of their health. Ten of them have died. Two were crushed by falling rocks, and eight were felled by weeks of unbearable work.

Those of us who are the Urban Company's slaves are for now doing mostly surface work. We're building industrial train tracks; we're digging; we're crushing rocks; we're pushing wagons; we're digging drainage ditches. One day we start the work here, another day there, seemingly at random. For now, a layman would have no idea just what it is we're building. But the engineers working among us insist that this will be a large-scale line of defense. Perhaps the Germans will be retreating this far back and so they're improvising a second Siegfried Line. All the work being done here is in preparation for an underground network of fortifications. Later on in Fürstenstein, I became convinced we were on the right track. As clear for all eyes to see, the grand duke's castle there was being rebuilt for use as a military headquarters.

That Hitler had materials and manpower in 1944, the fifth year of the war, for new Siegfried Lines wasn't a particularly uplifting thought. Appearances weren't at all in line with our only hope: the prospect of an imminent defeat.

And yet an underground nation of fortifications was emerging. That's what was being built. And not tentatively. Hundreds of thousands of deportees were spitting out their souls in the effort, and thousands of boxcars of wood, cement, and steel came pouring in. A frightening mass of entire SS and Wehrmacht regiments, divisions of Todt's people, civilian slave drivers, foremen, skilled laborers, miners, explosives experts, masons, mechanics, metalworkers, and carpenters sweated away among themselves and around every camp. Gradually Eule took on a new look.

Fresh human transports pull in one after another in the second half of June. First among them are a thousand deportees from Slovakia, Jews mostly from Košice and environs. Then come Poles, bestial-looking poor wretches who have been through pogroms, made the rounds of ghettos, and been in Nazi hands since 1939. Ten, twenty, or more of them drop dead each day, like flies. A group of several hundred people arrive from Transylvania, too. From Cluj-Napoca and Oradea. And then there are robust Jewish peasants from the Ukrainian Carpathians—deportees from Uzhhorod and Mukachevo. The melodic, drawling sounds of Yiddish now resound in the camp. Every company adds to its workforce. A new aristocracy is being born; new kapos, new Blockältesten, emerge.

The barracks are arising at a labored pace. By the end of July we all move into the new wood buildings. Each such twenty-four-room structure comprises a block, with its own Blockälteste in command. Bunkbeds and wood-chip mattresses await the prisoners. Thirty of us sleep in a room, and there are two of us to many of the beds, so the "comfort" here is not much greater than in the tents.

I myself become the resident of Block I, Room 5. My roommates are Ukrainian Jews from the Carpathian Mountains.

9

―

TWO HÄFTLINGE WITH THE SAME FAMILY NAME, WEISZ, have made the most successful "careers" in Eule. One of them—a squat, low-browed sales clerk from Upper Hungary—has become the Urban Company's chief kapo. He is the terror of his fellow men; more than a few vile murders of his brethren stain his soul. Later I heard that he'd been beaten to death in some camp even before the collapse. He never made it home.

He was an abominable go-getter, a brutishly cruel slave driver. A conscientious, even passionate implementer of the company's dark intentions. Filled with irrepressible energy, he was constantly making the rounds of work sites. True, his food was a thousand times better than ours. It came from the company kitchen, and he partook of every last privilege large and small meted out to the chosen apostates. This insidious, officious fellow was truly a "low-life Jew." He spoke Hungarian with some sort of peculiar, vile accent.

"Csinyáád vagy megdögőősz . . . !"—*"Do it, or you'll croak!"* he constantly rasped. Whenever he turned up somewhere with that rubber truncheon of his, our grips tightened on the pickaxes and spades we held, as if the camp commandant were approaching.

This power-crazed, malicious wild beast was a purebred

creation of the diabolically imaginative Nazi system, which was based on that old supposition—proven true on countless occasions—that the best slave driver is a slave accorded a privileged position. The bulk of the camp aristocracy was comprised of characters cut from the same cloth.

Uniquely, such towering figures of the Auschwitz hierarchy were recruited from among those who, back home, had stood on the bottom rungs of Jewish society. Those who'd made nothing of themselves—schnorrers, nebbishes, schlemiels, freeloaders, rogues, swindlers, idlers, slackers—all blossomed in this swamp.

At the same time—and this was the case with breathtaking regularity—those who back home had made respectable bourgeois careers for themselves, including industrialists, lawyers, wholesalers, and company executives, and those who'd inherited pews in houses of worship, here proved to be the most helpless of the lot. If that biblical saying "The last shall be first and the first last" was realized anywhere, it certainly was here: the last, the bums, became the first, and vice versa: those who'd been first, the respectable, the well-heeled, became the very last.

The other Weisz was an exception in many respects. His was the most envied role in the camp: caretaker at the supplies warehouse. He was called Pál; he had been a functionary back in Transylvania. Whether he survived this great cavalcade I don't know, but he had every opportunity to do so.

He'd landed in a singular situation indeed: able to do little favors for both the gray ones and Todt's people. He had the exclusive right to empty the ashtrays in the Todt people's offices, and he partook in no small measure in the soldiers' soup, which was graced with fat; he had a tin of tobacco, leather-soled work boots, a towel, a handkerchief, a pencil, and other treasures inaccessible to us. Moreover, he worked indoors and was treated somewhat like a human being. All this led him to wind up in circumstances so exceptional that his job, though it came with no distinguishing garb or title, was akin to that of any of the bigwigs—the difference being that he didn't even have to beat his comrades to stay in his position. Compared to this, little Bolgár's similar role seemed but modest luck.

Pál Weisz was a white raven among the many little gods. Sometimes he threw a bone at the throng of the nameless, even if he wasn't bound to them by any sense of kinship or camaraderie. I too am indebted to him for many comforting words and cigarettes.

Since the arrival of the newcomers, the situation has further deteriorated. We became a large camp indeed: there were already more than three thousand of us, and this was especially apparent from the dwindling of our food rations, which had been minimal to begin with. The all-powerful who distributed our bread and shares of Zulage stole ever more shamelessly. The kitchen barrack had been built, and the boilers were there, too, but no big new shipments of food arrived. That which came was still delivered by trucks in fifty-liter insulated cauldrons.

The first distribution was carried out by the Lagerälteste and his assistants. They handed out rations to each block. Within a block, the Blockälteste would distribute to the rooms, and finally we could access food by way of the room commander. Much was misappropriated through all those sticky hands. The allotment of twenty grams of fat per person we'd originally gotten every day, above all to maintain life, shrank to microscopic bits.

Max, the Lagerälteste, that derelict from Paris, was given to unbearable rampages. As for the Appells, their chief attraction was barbarous caning. SS men, Todt's people, civilian supervisors, and häftling chieftains were vying to see who could torment us the most. There was but a surreal semblance of life among our mushrooming numbers in the barracks.

Maurer, too, no longer stuck to his guns. The kilos he'd brought with him from home finally faded away, and the once stout, heavy man became a shadow of himself.

"I take back everything," he declared despondently. "This really can't be endured for four months."

All told, two months had passed. Technically summer had come, but the weather—as if conspiring with genocide—just didn't want to make a lasting turn for the better. The clouds were wandering indefatigably over the Silesian sky, rain kept gushing down, and, like sprinkled flour, specks of frost still coated the landscape on those forlorn dawns.

We are begrimed once and for all, irrevocably so. Long gone is that sandy bit of soap handed to us on arrival, and our underwear has stuck in filthy shreds to our paupers' rags, whose colors are unrecognizable. The soles of our wooden shoes have come off, so it is with wounded bare feet that we squelch along all day long through mud that covers everything.

As a logical culmination, all at once, body lice appear. Palm-size encampments of glittering larvae take shape in our rags and blankets. Like the turbulent images in a nightmare, these silvery splotches begin to stir, then squirm, and then frightfully, inextinguishably, disperse. Our nights of half sleep end, like that. Those hours allotted to rest now pass with curses and tormented scratching. Despite the risk of meeting with the slave drivers' rubber truncheons and the sentry's rifle butt, even during the day we have no choice: we repeatedly set down our tools to scratch ourselves all over, our faces contorted with rage.

The pseudo-doctor with apathy written all over his face has become the camp's head doctor. There are lots of genuine doctors among the new internees, and a few of them manage to land positions in his office. One of the bigwigs persuaded Max that a camp this big can't be without a *Krankenstube*—an infirmary. The Lagerälteste intervened, and finally some twenty pallets were freed up for the dying, those who'd been cudgeled half to death, and those who'd otherwise met with misfortune. Some of our new doctors succeeded in finding their way into the paradise of the Krankenstube as medics.

Of course there are no medications, bandages, or medical equipment, so effective intervention is impossible. Only those at death's door can be admitted. No one emerges healed from the Krankenstube, which begins to take on the trappings of a veritable death row. We do our best to go nowhere near it. Fortunately, so far there have been no cases of typhus. The prevailing opinion is that lice aren't as infectious in spring and summer.

By now the dead are pouring out of the Krankenstube, but even at work sites it's now a daily occurrence that some häftling drops dead. Special units of camp workers throw the corpses into giant lime pits dug outside the camp. Using pliers, the Polish head doctor first breaks loose the corpses' gold teeth. After collecting a hefty toll on the amassed gold and dividing the bounty with the Lagerälteste, he "turns in" the remainder to the camp commandant. As a result, all parties get their hands on decent supplemental income. This is more or less the same practice at all camps.

Only two months have passed, and our ranks have already

frighteningly thinned out. Among my acquaintances the first to go is Freund, that puny fellow who'd run a handicraft shop. With excruciating agony, an intestinal illness did him in. Kende, the sanguine bald accountant, follows him. The previous day he held a half-hour presentation about his little girl—his little girl, whom he adored. He described the moment when they would see each other again. Bokor, from Novi Sad, winds up in the lime pit dreadfully bloated, and others, around ten or twenty at a time, with whom I am only passingly familiar. The last days of June see a record harvest of death. It seems that dragging people away to hard labor who are not accustomed to such physical exertion and who'd been raised in other life circumstances is not a particularly profitable enterprise for the Germans.

Here muscle counts. The SS guards are hunkered down ominously at the work sites. It's strictly prohibited for them to commingle with the slaves. The work is in fact overseen by the company's civilian foreman, the Meister. There's a sharp divide between the jurisdiction of the sentry on the one hand and the Meister on the other. The former is responsible for ensuring that the häftlinge should not escape while working outside of the barbed wire. But there are some among them who, driven by a sense of personal diligence or else by boredom, partake in the slave driving as well. Most of the guards are young men. It is a depressing thought that the Nazis are still in such good shape that they can do without this manpower on the front.

The sentries are constantly being replaced. Each work site sees new ones daily. The authorities take utmost care to ensure that not even the most superficial human contact or relationship can sprout between guard and guarded. It is in vain that we look for signs of commiseration or sympathy on the faces of our guards. Generally speaking, whether soldiers or civilians, these people obviously don't lend more than a passing thought to the question of who, after all, are these haggard, starving, ragged wretches, who've been dragged here so far from their homes.

I'm convinced that the average Nazi who had dealings with us imagines, more or less, that standing there before them are a bunch of ex-convicts, common criminals, and that every Jew had notched up at least one murder. Perhaps—for the sake of simplicity—they have been taught to believe exactly this sort of thing.

I remember just one exception. Herman, an SS private and a bartender from Breslau. A pear-faced, dreadfully thin fellow. He did not stare at us with the ferocious hatred of the others. My God . . . He'd been a bartender. . . . Perhaps a bartender can't hate even when thrust into an SS uniform. Quite a few times I worked in units Herman was guarding. He would always try to start up a conversation with one of us, and, like the biblical sower of seeds, would regularly drop a burning cigarette he'd just started, right in front of us. I too reaped Herman's gifts. Resounding in me even now is the happiness that welled up inside when I picked up that cigarette and looked at the conspiratorial smile on that pear-shaped face of his. A whole, well-stuffed cigarette. . . . Enough to roll into six thin ones, so that bewitching sense of home cast by nicotine's magic would be mine six times over.

In the course of later events, I often thought of Herman, the bartender from Breslau. He became a firm, comforting presence in my memory amid the upheaval that was to come.

This Herman was our guard the day Half Arm appeared. Slaves and slave drivers alike were panic-stricken. The alarming news passed from one group to the next: Half Arm is here!

In no time we learned who he was from those who came here before us and had survived a few of his inspections. So then, Half Arm was the chief supervisor of the Gross-Rosen network of camps. An SS captain, he wore one of his arms in a sling, owing to a wound from the front. During his previous visit he'd shot two people and lashed out a few times with his whip at nearly every person he walked past. Ten or twelve miserable wretches accidentally drew attention to themselves. He shoved them to the ground, and he then spent several minutes stomping on their bellies. Even the SS sentries had it coming. Half Arm found fault everywhere, and liberally sentenced people to solitary confinement.

That happened three months ago, before our arrival. And now he's here again.

"Oy vey!" the Poles murmur throughout the camp. The rest of us wait to see what would happen. That day I was at work digging drainage ditches about 150 to 200 meters from the camp. I was heaving rocky yellow earth from a deep pit into a rail cart, but first I had to break up the soil with a pickax. It was hard work, but even on that day Herman didn't leave me in the lurch. He dropped his gift into my pit, this time a little bag of makhorka, a coarse Ukrainian tobacco.

With a lit cigarette hanging from between my lips, I was able to take in even the horror stories about Half Arm with composure. I regarded all the agitated scurrying to be hysteria. What more could happen, after all? We were outside the protection of the law every hour of every day anyway, within shooting range of murderers.

The camp veterans were right, after all. Half Arm was something else. Instead of our everyday gray hell, thunderbolts of striking, kitschy drama.

He arrived in a camp automobile. His left arm was swaddled in a thick white sling, with black silk binding on top. Under the flat-topped cap with the death's-head emblem on the front, a fine, professorial skull. A cigarette was smoldering between straight, slender lips. Thin gold-framed spectacles atop a finely cut nose.

An SS captain, with numerous decorations. Murderer, made in Germany. He has a college degree, and perhaps he can play Bach passably on the piano.

He emerges from the vehicle with the camp commandant and two officers I don't recognize. Our everyday executioner shrinks into himself in the shadow of the higher power. One of the officers has a sparkling Leica camera in his hands. He is taking pictures of the site. Herman gives a report. Half Arm, the despot presiding over several hundred thousand people, a whole network of camps, steps slowly, indifferently, among us.

By now no one is looking up. Physical exertion is our escape. Fingers curl tighter than ever around the pickaxes, earth comes crashing down wildly into the rail carts, and those pushing the carts press their whole bodies up against them. The tiny carts screech as they race along the lurching, narrow rails.

"Kapo!" calls out Half Arm.

Most of the men in our group are from Uzhhorod and Muka-chevo. They were manual laborers back home, too. Tradesmen, haulers, lumberjacks, loaders. They work well. They can't even work badly. The tools themselves sweep them along.

The kapo, who is also of this stock, is pale as he springs

forward. As proscribed, he snatches off his round, prisoner's cap, the *Schmützen*. His whole body is trembling, but he stands at taut attention.

"How's the work going, kapo?"

Half Arm's words are almost friendly. He doesn't raise his voice at all. Not even a commanding tone. This tall figure of a man with one arm in a sling looks down upon the slave. The ragged striped linen trousers hang helplessly, loosely, on the junior kapo. Now we also glance up.

"I humbly report that the work is progressing well."

He speaks German with a strong Yiddish accent. Half Arm nods approvingly.

"*Schön* [Nice].Who is your best worker?"

"46514!" the kapo exclaims without hesitation.

46514 is inarguably the group's best worker. Back home he'd been a logger. Twenty-six years old. Nothing of his round, sunburnt peasant's face suggests Jewish ancestry. Not at all the spindly, bookish type more familiar back home. That variation that even Jews themselves hardly recognize. In the Carpathian Mountains, there's a healthier degree of occupational diversity among the Jews. Those doing work do it for the sake of the work itself. It's obvious from the way they hold their tools.

46514 is a premium häftling. Premiums are rare; to be recognized as one is a big deal. A premium gets a weekly bonus worth two marks, which he can trade in for special jam and makhorka cigarettes.

46514 jumps out of the pit and snatches off his cap.

Half Arm casts him a glance but asks him nothing, and then steps to the side. He reaches lazily for his holster, pulls out the revolver, and presses the barrel to 46514's temple. A shot rings out. The man, who'd been standing straight as a flagpole, now teeters before crashing facedown into the pit.

The lifeless body plops with a dull thud. The officer with the Leica puts the camera into a pocket, while Half Arm smiles silently, absentmindedly.

"A little demonstration," he says. "An example of how even the best Jew must croak."

Kitsch. Horror is always kitsch. Even when it's real.

Half Arm puts away the revolver and gets back into the car with his entourage. Fifteen steps away from us, 46514's ever-colder lips are caressing the curse-soaked earth gone mad.

The car rumbles off, and the Meister hounds us in his usual voice:

"*Los!* . . . *Bewegung!* [Come on! . . . Move!]"

The pickaxes start swinging, and the rail carts jolt into motion.

It's June 6, 1944, the day of the Allied landing on the coast of France.

10

THE INVASION ON THE WESTERN FRONT SOON BROUGHT a new regimen to Eule, as well, one even more inhumane than we had experienced until then. The coercion ratcheted up, and four-fifths of the camp residents now worked underground. Baugesellschaft, the company that had been building the barracks, ceased its operations here, and with that the opportunity for relatively favorable work disappeared. Its workforce was absorbed by Kemna and Urban. German bombers and helicopters buzzed about over the camp.

The multitude of barracks was complete. We'd become a mid-size provincial city of the Land of Auschwitz. Roads were taking shape here, as elsewhere, as were a main square, a cemetery, a latrine, and a place of execution—the hubs of the cities of death. The kitchen stood ready but was not in operation, since necessary food supplies were still late in arriving. The trucks brought swill more wretched by the day. The quarter loaf of bread shrank to a fifth. The cost of tobacco shot up sky-high. There was nothing to smoke anymore. The Greeks, those swindling magicians, wrung out an entire daily ration of food for a single makhorka cigarette that sputtered out in seconds. Extra pay—supplemental rations—ceased, and with it the main source of currency with which to acquire other goods. Nor did we happen upon any more English POWs at the train station, who sometimes complemented their cordial hellos by letting a Caporal cigarette or two fall to the ground. It seemed that the Tommies had been led away from our region.

As the Zulage thinned out, milk soup and potatoes in sauce, our two "festive" courses, vanished from our menu. Instead, ever more often we were given boiled potato skins, "food" that even animals would have rejected with disgust.

Dried out, shriveled to the bone, and full of painful boils, we dragged ourselves about. Indifferently, we received news of the mounting numbers of deaths. We got to the point where we began dreaming up escape plans, even though common sense told us it was unimaginable that in such a condition and attire we'd make it even five hundred meters beyond the barbed wire.

The sixteen-year-old Greek kid who'd somehow struggled over the barbed wire one night was caught by dawn hiding inside a guardhouse. The boy was not finished off at Eule. He was dealt with in pomp and circumstance. They painted on the back of his häftling jacket, in ungainly red letters: Flüchtling [Escapee].* Then they locked him in a windowless cement shed for three days without food or water. On the fourth day, two machine-pistol-toting SS guards came and took him to Gross-Rosen, the district center. There could not be a shred of doubt as to his fate.

All this did not deter us. Even those with the most common sense had fallen into the grips of a sort of suicidal despair. I

---

* The German *Flüchtling* typically translates as "refugee," whereas *Ausbrecher* is "escapee." Debreczeni writes *Flüchtling* and then the Hungarian word *szökevény* (escapee).

think there couldn't have been more than a hundred completely sound-minded prisoners among us in those days.

That's when Feldmann, a onetime officer with the general staff of the Czechoslovakian army, stepped to the stage. His barrack became our secret meeting place after Appells. This man with military bearing and graying hair had held himself together with remarkable strength. He radiated an inextinguishable life force. He was perhaps in the best physical condition among the three thousand häftlinge there. He'd attained a minor office, having been named junior kapo at one of the tunnel labor units.

By the time Maurer initiated me, more than one hundred people were already gathering daily in Feldmann's barrack. The meetings had a beneficial effect upon the downhearted people. First and foremost, the onetime general staff officer assessed the news from the front that came from little Bolgár and Pál Weisz. Feldmann improvised maps as he held presentations about peoples who become masters of their fate and of the things they can achieve. This gave us a glimpse of the life that perhaps awaited even us, and for which it was worth galvanizing our sporadically beating hearts and flagging strength for the struggle to persist.

There were no sharply political speeches staking out positions. No, we weren't up for much analysis and debate, for indeed we'd become creatures of instinct, above all, in the grips of animal, primal desires: to eat, to stretch out, to rest, to smoke cigarettes. . . . I'm certain the vast majority of us didn't think too much even about our families.

By no means were Feldmann's séance-like gatherings similar, or could they have been similar to the organizing activities at prisoner-of-war camps, in which the participants consciously and systematically prepared for their futures. Compared to us, the residents of POW camps were carefree vacationers.

No matter how nascent and clumsy this effort, in effect, at least momentarily, it was a medicine. Vázsonyi, Maurer, Gleiwitz, Grosz, Bolgár, Weisz, I myself, and all of us who were still more or less in our right minds spoke up, or, lying on pallets, listened to the words voiced in that dark coop. The talking unfolded in Hungarian, but we translated what was said into Polish and—in the interest of the few among us from the west—sometimes also into German.

One evening Feldmann got down to specifics. He made a formal proposal.

"Most all of us understand," he said, "that with the invasion having taken place, events will accelerate. At this moment, especially amid our circumstances, it's impossible to foretell the degree of this acceleration, and how it will be manifested. One thing's certain: we mustn't find ourselves unprepared for a possible quick turn of events. There's just one way of doing this: to join forces."

He set forth his plan in detail. The initial participants will organize themselves into cells of ten. The cells will stir up the others. Each member of a cell will organize another group of thirty people. The Greeks will not be included. In the event of indisputable signs that liberating forces were drawing near, at a given signal we will try breaking out. True, we were unarmed and weak, but there were three thousand of us up against two hundred SS guards. Everyone will know that this was about life, and that fierce determination will boost our strength many times over. The first weapons will need to be acquired by surprise attacks on isolated guard posts.

It was a desperate thought, but there was in fact no other choice. This seemed to be the only possible means of heading off what we assumed would be the Nazis' move—that in the event of danger, they would destroy the camp, prisoners and all.

We all accepted the plan. With that, however, the whole embryonic effort came to an end. Never could we get around to executing the plan, to even stir up the others, because three days later two-thirds of the camp were led away and sent packing. Naturally, that was it for Feldmann's séances, and the escape plan fell through.

It so happened that the big news was announced at the evening Appell following the very meeting at which Feldmann shared his plan.

After routine business was out of the way—which is to say, the merciless caning of "offenders"—Max stepped to the center with the clerk.

"I'll be reading out numbers," he declared. "Those who hear their number will not join their division tomorrow morning but stand in a separate column."

Everyone shuddered with fear. What could this mean? We didn't like being marked as different; we dreaded standing out in any way.

It took two hours for all the numbers to be read out. Even after the signal for curfew, Max kept bellowing steadfastly. Almost two thousand people had been designated. I was at the very beginning of the list. *Should I be happy or scared?* What was clear from the outset was that we were leaving this place. Surely I couldn't end up in a place much worse, I thought—and how tragically wrong I was. The worst-case scenario was Birkenau, with its forest of billowing chimneys. And that, if I thought about it, wasn't such an objectionable solution.

The next morning, we set off on foot with two days of bread rations. Wonder of wonders, Max, the dreaded camp god, was also among us. Our hated Lagerälteste had fallen victim to a state coup. The brains behind the coup were Weisz, the Urban Company kapo, and Michel, the shifty clerk. They'd compiled the list completely at random. Meanwhile they managed to denounce Max to the commandant. They'd persuaded the butcher to force him out, too.

Hellish irony—in hell.

Max reads out the numbers in a booming voice. All at once he happens upon his own. He must call that out, too; there's no appeal. In the blink of an eye this Parisian brothel owner, this murderer and renegade, is demoted to an ordinary häftling. But not quite entirely, after all: the camp commandant had shown mercy, appointing his disgraced henchman as kapo of our departing unit.

Where to? This was on the minds of each of us. The two days of bread rations suggested a long march, and the large number of accompanying SS guards and Todt's people was not an encouraging sign.

Indeed, a long march ensued, as so often before during our time in this accursed land. It was our bare feet we dragged along, since the wooden shoes we'd gotten at Auschwitz had long since wound up in the trash. Nor did the well-maintained asphalt roads we now trod upon bring much relief to our bloodied, wounded feet. Of course, everyone gobbled down the two days' worth of bread rations right after it was handed out. A famished häftling can never keep his jaw muscles sufficiently under control to evenly apportion his food.

On this occasion—for the slave, when it rains it pours—even the sun was out to prove itself a real man. Stalwartly it blazed down upon us, steaming our rags in dust and sweat. In the meantime, the lice were busy with their painful work.

Again, we passed by camps, and tiny ghost towns came and went. Our first stop was toward evening on a steep little road in a quiet town. One group after another, we were led into a building that turned out to be the local public bath. Once more we had to cast our clothes into a heap. We stood under showers as our rags were deloused. By the time they chased us out of that paradise of hot water, naturally no one could find their own rags among those that had been thrown back into a jumbled mess that all looked the same. We had to struggle mightily for every piece. After that fistfight, I found myself in worse rags than ever before. Until then I'd sought to maintain at least my shirt and underwear as much as possible, but now instead of those I got only scraps.

That is how, the following evening, we arrived at a new station: in front of the barbed wire of Hitler's *Arbeitslager*—labor camp—in Fürstenstein, bearing the Roman number III.

Part II

11

<hr/>

A HUGE CASTLE ENCIRCLED BY A MAGNIFICENT PARK OF two thousand acres looks down silently, all-knowingly, upon six long rows of round green tents; on a machine gun–equipped watchtower; on the tangled course of the barbed wire fence; and on the other typical characteristics of death camps. Fürstenstein is the headquarters of a onetime German aristocratic family, the Fürstenstein-Pless dynasty. The camp has obviously been built here because of the imposing 450-room, four-story castle. As indicated by the inscription engraved into the marble façade above its main gate, this architectural wonder of the Middle Ages was restored at the end of the nineteenth century, but aside from the middle, residential wing, its exterior was left in its original form. Polygonal projecting corner turrets of raw stone and bastions interlaid with portholes safeguard the ambience of the Middle Ages. Naturally, not of those Middle Ages that Hitler's lunatics imposed in the forties of the twentieth century, but veritably one much more humane. In those Middle Ages in which these stones looked out upon knights and noblewomen, there were still serfs, but in Europe, at least, slavery was no more.

Today's living scion of the Fürstenstein-Pless family, it's said, married an Englishwoman and fled Hitler by immigrating to

London. Presumably he's still there. And yet Hitler's strategy sentenced the gorgeous structure to death. Within days, hundreds of rooms packed with priceless frescoes, artistic furniture, and ornaments were destroyed. Legions of German and Ukrainian workers, as well as thousands of Jewish deportees, were kept busy ravaging the place night and day. They broke down walls and smashed to dust the wide-eyed angels that had been painted on them. Haughty bastions crumbled under iron pickaxes.

In the huge park, they began drying out the artificial lake and destroying whole swaths of forest. Silky manicured lawns were torn up by a rusty industrial rail line, and a chaotic mass of ditches and pits rendered gravel paths unwalkable.

Vast underground spaces now stretched out under the ancient structure. Networks of veritable catacombs were being expanded for kilometers in length and depth.

A zigzagging underground city was undoubtedly being built. So the notion that this would just keep expanding all over the place, that we were in the heart of the new, large-scale line of defense, seemed fairly credible; the castle, along with its constituent parts, was being rebuilt for use as Hitler's main military headquarters in the event of a retreat, and vital weapon-manufacturing facilities would be placed within this city of caves.

All two thousand of us were here to supplement the existing army of workers, which was imposing enough on its own.

So it's not the gas chamber. It's a life of slavery. Uninterrupted. I take notice of this certitude with no particular sense of satisfaction. I am not enthusiastic about the continued series of days that promise not a thing, that achieve not a thing. Two days of marching in hunger, in thirst, and in rags is considerable enough an interval of time to befriend the thought of a quick death.

Our first impression is not exactly uplifting. The camp is much bigger than Eule. It reached a population of four thousand even before our arrival, and yet the relative comfort of barracks is nowhere to be seen. To again sink into the unbearable stench of the wood-framed tents is not a rosy prospect in and of itself, but when I see the first tent in Fürstenstein I start imagining Eule as a lost paradise.

After our arrival, forty, sometimes even fifty people are crammed into tents intended to house twenty-four. Few of them are empty. We newcomers have popped into our fellow sufferers' lives as uninvited, not at all welcome guests.

I wind up in Number 28, the most notorious tent. Its residents are under quarantine. The common criminals who live here—naturally, they are Jews, too—were deported to Auschwitz from the Kőhíd penitentiary on the outskirts of Sopron, in western Hungary. As for my assigned quarters, I'm not in luck. To be placed among forty wily, cynical scoundrels ready for anything is more than unfortunate.

These prisoners were sentenced to many long years for murder, burglary, and dealing in stolen goods. There's not even a single white-collar criminal in 28. Their time behind bars has shriveled up their remaining humanity. It doesn't take much to imagine the savagery into which they've descended, and the passions with which they welcome newcomers, on account of whom they must squeeze together even more, as others commandeer a portion of their tiny lairs.

Our room commander is Sanyi Róth, a notorious repeat

offender. A serial burglar, he'd been serving a four-year sentence at the start of the German occupation.

His associates are flagrant refutations of the Nazis' vehement espousal of a theory of a distinct Jewish race. There's no Jewishness in them; born criminality, for sure.

I find myself in Tent 28 starting on the night of our arrival. Aside from me, only little Bolgár ends up in the "Markó." This is the nickname—referring to Budapest's infamous Markó Street Prison—of my home-to-be.

Sanyi Róth sizes me up with disgust.

"Who the hell let you two loose here?"

Little Bolgár replies unsuspectingly:

"The Lageräteste, I think. Judging from his armband, that's what he probably was."

"He can go drop dead along with both of you! That pig no doubt wasn't handing out new cigars in the gentlemen's tents, huh? And yet there are twenty-four to a tent stretched out there."

"Make some room for us to lie down, comrades," I say.

Scornful laughter and sarcastic comments emanate from the tent.

"You honorable gentlemen wish to have some rest, do you? Even lying down? Sitting won't do?"

We look about. There's clearly something to what they're saying: it's impossible to imagine that they'll make room for the newcomers in this pigsty.

Fortunately, the deputy Lageräteste looks in just then—a pudgy, ever-shouting character. He's here to confirm that the newcomers are given space. That's when a miracle happens. The natives of Number 28 gruffly and yet obediently draw their own lairs closer together. They are evidently scared of the bellowing little man whose voice carries as if he were training savages.

Somehow we manage to set down our blankets. Not that we get food even now, since we arrived having been "provided for" for two days. The others now get their share. The prisoners of Number 28 are snatching at the bread thrown their way. Deep within the tent four men are grappling desperately, grinding their teeth. There's one loaf of bread to every four prisoners, and the fighters can't come to terms despite their diligent measuring right down to the centimeter. Arguments are constantly erupting into hand-to-hand combat over who gets the more substantial ends of the loaves.

Without so much as looking, Róth swings a plank down among them, whereupon silence ensues. One of the struggling men staggers to his feet brutishly, his forehead bleeding, and casts a hollow stare upon his piece of bread. He takes an eager bite and gobbles it down.

I rub my burning and yet heavy eyes. This is new territory, even after Eule. Where have I wound up? My glance meets little Bolgár's teary eyes.

Practically everyone in the tent is chewing noisily, slurping, squealing. They're moaning away while wallowing in the fodder, as if copulating. Róth produces a grimy lamp and places it carefully on the wooden shelf nailed above the pallets. A stuporous, stunted band of light pans the space. A prop in some Gorky play.

Our room commander is munching on a kohlrabi. He laughs.

"I freed up a mere three of them, two kilos apiece."

He reaches up to the shelf and pulls the treasure out of his wooden crate.

"Where?" come several voices at once.

"Behind the kitchen. They brought them yesterday. Margarine, cabbage, and beets came in, too. The kitchen staff are going crazy gorging themselves."

Eyes full of envy but also reverence follow the path of that kohlrabi into Sanyi Róth's gaping mouth.

"You snuck out to the kitchen?"

"Blockhead! I've been working there for two days. We're washing kettles. Easy gig."

"Lucky devil," says his neighbor with almost tender recognition.

"Hell no," says Róth in a swaggering tone. "If I really was, I'd now have a quarter pack of margarine. Man, I got into the first kitchen today with two kettles. There's no one about. The grub is on the table. And I hesitate, like an idiot. The next thing I know, the potato kapo comes in and kicks me in the ass. If only that devil had come by a second later . . . Ah. . . ."

"How many portions is a quarter pack?"

"At least twenty."

Tent 28 is daydreaming. Rosy fingers tickle the fantasies preprogrammed to imagine gastronomic images. *Twenty portions of margarine . . .*

Here there is no yakking away about some utopian future, as in Eule. Little Bolgár's battlefield explications would find little interest. The brutishness is a degree deeper. Tent 28 is no longer dreaming of liberation.

They barely even notice us for now. My neighbor stretches out spitefully beside me. I can hardly breathe, but protesting seems inadvisable at the moment. Goings-on in the camp are being debated: unfamiliar names are flung about; unfamiliar events are flaring tempers. Cursing away, they speak of a tunnel and of a night shift, and they list the dead.

Finally, Róth sees us, too.

"Do you have cigarettes?"

"They have lice," one of the longtime residents replied instead of us.

Róth snaps at him:

"Did I ask you, Jaksi?"

Jaksi, a young guy whose face is full of zits, cowers. The room commander now addresses me directly:

"Where did you two come from?"

"From Eule."

"Where's that?"

"I don't know. We walked for two days."

"What cities did you come through?"

"Waldenburg was the only one whose name I noticed."

"What was the camp like?"

"Terrible."

"A third or a quarter loaf of bread?"

"A quarter."

"Did you get bonus food, too?"

"Sometimes."

"Work? Treatment?"

"Terrible."

The strapping white-haired man now says more quietly:

"Well, you'll see a thing or two here, too."

We did. The next day. The atmosphere at the early-morning Appell was even more hopeless than in Eule. We flounder through the pitch-black dark in ankle-deep slush between the tents toward the gate. That's where the lineup is.

Ältesten and kapos are running about. Their tools of notification and persuasion—rubber truncheons—thud away. The prisoners here are even more ragged than we are, if that's possible. But perhaps it only seems that way. The copious scratching of the pitter-pattering shadows reveals that lice aren't scarce here, either.

The kapos hustle the people into their groups. Arms crossed, the big bosses contemplate the chaos in front of Tent 1, the joint residence of the Lägeraltesten and the clerks. Commands are crackling in both German and Hungarian, identifying the companies utilizing the slave labor:

"Hegerfeld, antreten [Hegerfeld, line up]*!"*

"Lagerarbeiter zu mir [Camp workers come to me]*!"*

"Sänger und Lanninger! Sänger und Lanninger! [*"*Sänger and Lanninger! Sänger and Lanninger!]*"*

"Pischl munkások felállni [Pischl workers to your feet]*!"*

"Kemnások! Kemnások! Első utca! [Kemna workers! Kemna workers! First street!]*"*

"Tegnap érkezettek! Újak! Hozzám! [Those who arrived yesterday! Newcomers! Get over here!]*"*

Well-ordered columns form out of frenzied maelstroms.

We stand in a separate group. Two häftlinge are approaching us from the ranks of the big bosses. A fortyish or fiftyish fat man with a goodly cudgel, and a clean-shaven bald young man. The top Lägeralteste and the clerk. The kapos bark:

"Achtung! Schmützen ab! [Attention! Caps off!]*"*

Caps fly off heads in front of those two cleanly clothed and freshly washed kapo-slaves who are approaching. In Fürstenstein, standing taut, at attention, is due not only the Germans but also the head slave drivers among the Jews.

Flailing a cudgel, Berkovits, Fürstenstein's top Lagerälteste, is more dreaded than even Max was back in Eule. For his part, Max, in charge of the newcomers, is running to and fro in front of us, shouting and gesticulating, making order. Like some forlorn ax without wood to cut, he is striving to suck up enough to the big bosses to achieve at least a mid-level rank. No one knows him here, and he knows no one.

With forced impartiality, he steps before Berkovits and says in a tone of fraternal informality:

"Allow me, colleague . . . sir. I am Max, Lagerälteste."

With that cudgel of his, Berkovits unhesitatingly strikes the hand extended toward him. Max gasps in pain and steps back in shock. A murmur of hushed fainthearted chuckling arises from our group, though we really aren't in the mood for laughter. We are witnesses to a classic example of poetic justice.

"There are only two of us Ältesten here. Those who don't get that, we'll deal with them. *Verstanden* [Understand]?"

Max cowers. He tries saving what can be salvaged.

"But in Eule I was appointed the kapo of this newly arrived group."

"Kapo—maybe that can be considered. We'll see."

Berkovits is from Upper Hungary. A shadowy figure, he is said to have been a merchant. He served a long time for bankruptcy fraud. He is a textbook case of the twisted laws on how to make something of oneself in a camp. He applies his authority fully. It's said that he and Röhmer, the clerk from Czechoslovakia, who happens to be an engineer, have the camp commander fully in their grips.

Now this Röhmer also steps up to us. He has a list in his hands. He is speaking German. He reads out our numbers and assigns us to the already-formed groups. I wind up among the Sänger und Lanninger men. I take my place in the long line. My neighbor—a stooped, pale man—says in a hushed voice:

"So, you really did well."

"Why?"

"You know what Sänger und Lanninger means?"

"No."

"The worst tunnel. You'll see."

"Can *you* endure it?"

"Only Kemna is worse than Sänger und Lanninger," he says instead of answering, with deep conviction. "And hell. You're from Budapest?"

"Bačka."

"They dragged me off from Budapest. They took me off Tram Forty-Four by the Keleti Train Station. My name was Farkas. Dr. Farkas."

I too say my onetime name. For the first time since I've been here. We shake hands.

In the time it takes for us to reach the work site four kilometers away, Dr. Farkas, the Budapest physician, shows me Fürstenstein. He speaks of Sänger und Lanninger and its slaves. This company is building the subterranean world of caverns. Back-breaking, soul-crushing labor. The blasting, drilling, and carrying out of rocks unfolds incessantly twenty-four hours straight in two shifts. The operations are overseen by Italian skilled workers. Followers of Prime Minister Pietro Badoglio. Prisoners of war and internees. They wound up in German hands after Mussolini's downfall. Italians are supposedly the best tunnel workers.

Sänger und Lanninger is a private company. Its headquarters is in Berlin or perhaps Düsseldorf. Here, in Fürstenstein, it maintains a well-staffed regional center. It works for the state and pays its shareholders decent dividends. Here, however, twenty to thirty outcasts a day drop dead while the enterprise pursues profit. The onetime East India Company and the tea magnates of Ceylon were more interested in the fates of the slaves that toiled away on their plantations than the shareholders of Sänger und Lanninger are in our lot. We weren't even the property of these undoubtedly distinguished financiers and entrepreneurs. Our disappearance meant not the least financial loss to them. To the state, even less so. There was plenty of material.

The company's top resident slave driver is the chief engineer. A typical German: glowing hot with the fury of work and with hatred. Victory and profit are equally important to him. Driven by this dual ideal, he too does some driving. With an effective method at that. What with his feathered green hunting hat and his ill-tailored tight Hubertus hunting trousers, he is like a caricature from the pages of the Munich weekly magazine *Fliegende Blätter*. But he emanates an atmosphere of terror akin to that of Half Arm, the slave driver from Gross-Rosen.

No, Green Hat doesn't kill with his own hands. After all, murder isn't among the duties of a chief engineer on a regular salary. He doesn't even strike anyone. Instead, he prepares lists, takes notes. Tirelessly he walks through the underground shafts, amid the drills' raging noise, coming up unnoticed behind the häftling:

"Please give me your number!" says Green Hat to the slave, who had perhaps paused at that very moment to catch a breath.

Yes, he addresses us with a measure of civility. He takes notes, and without a word he goes on. But the recorded numbers end up with the camp commandant and are called out at the Appell for caning. Green Hat sometimes hands over twenty or thirty numbers.

Now I am a tunnel worker. Cave networks are expanding along the entire length of the ridge surrounding the castle. The quartz hillside is pockmarked with ten mine shafts. In the belly of the hill are long, ever longer corridors that widen into rooms and halls small and large, as well as veritable squares. The caves are connected by cross passages.

Tunneling is hard work. That much I knew even before. All over the world, laborers battling underground with homicidal rocks are well paid and provided with special care. Here the guiding principle is the opposite of all that.

Swaying hand-carried lamps and dirty lightbulbs hanging from jutting rocks barely mitigate the oppressive darkness. The drills scream away as they bore into the walls; slabs of rock hundreds of kilograms apiece crash to the ground; and the ceiling crumbles. Like megaphones, echoes amplify the rumble of the little carts packed with crushed rocks.

Bone-piercing humidity every which way. Dampness radiates from the rocks and oozes under our feet from the sodden ground.

In some places concrete is already being laid, and elsewhere sacks are being carried for the insatiable bellies of the cement mixers. Beams are being dragged along; shadows are swaying on multilevel scaffolding. This was the first time I worked in a tunnel. In Eule, I managed to avoid it, but now, it seems, I have plunged in irrevocably.

The kapo cups his hands by his mouth:

"You'll be carrying *Bohre. Los* [Come on]!"

"Fortune amid misfortune," says Farkas beside me like an *Amen* on hearing this. "Take care to stay in this role!"

I have no idea what *Bohre* means, and asking questions seems inadvisable. Fortunately, Farkas fills me in, before whizzing past me with a loaded cart.

Bohre are iron rods of varying lengths that are chisel shaped at both ends. Layer by layer, these electrically powered chisels break slabs off the rock walls previously loosened by blasting. A *Bohre* can be used for only a couple of minutes, since the blades quickly get dull. They are then taken to the blacksmith shop, forged, and rehammered.

From scaffold to scaffold I stumble along collecting the used rods. In some spots the Italians all but fling them on my head. I heave four or five of the rods onto my shoulder and clamber out into the sunlight. I go another fifty or so meters uphill to the blacksmith shop. An SS guard is watching me from behind. Once there, I pick up the newly forged rods and head back in. So it goes, nonstop, through the whole day of toil.

Undoubtedly, this privileged position isn't fit for moles as much as lugging rocks all day underground, but that doesn't mean it's child's play in the least. And yet it's not mine for long. Only a few days later I'm demoted, and from then on for many months I'm clambering in the army of pariahs hauling rocks.

Of course there's not a trace of safety precautions at the workplaces. Rockfalls are frequent, and rare is the day that does not see one or two crushed-to-death häftlinge carried out of some shaft.

Such images are to be expected. Neither slave drivers nor slaves so much as glance at the corpses. Motor vehicles run down many people. Trucks packed full of sand, cement, bricks, slag, and beams roll in one after another, piling up in this tight space flanked by heaps of sand and rock. häftlinge are often pulled from under their wheels. Not in a single case is there a report or investigation. Running down a häftling carries not the slightest consequence, just the same as if the driver had driven over a dog or a goose.

There are also some victims who wind up under the wheels not quite unintentionally. Why not, after all? A faster and easier opportunity for suicide rarely presented itself.

Both the gray ones and the Italian mine specialists, who aren't much for talking but are for hitting, enjoy the bloodcurdling scenes. Sometimes they even crack a joke about it:

"Well, Jews, won't anyone kill himself today? I want to see a corpse."

At times they even help along a waverer with an inconspicuous shove. Just for the fun of it.

Little by little the dungeons of Fürstenstein make me feel lousy. Literally so—infested with lice, that is. Washing up and disinfecting loses its effect on the first day. Those who've been here awhile are much lousier than we are. In general, everything is one or two degrees worse than in Eule: the food, the workplaces, the health-care situation, the hierarchy. The last of these is far more complicated here. Since there is a separate kitchen, a privileged caste of food workers has developed. Instead of just one Lagerälteste, or Camp Elder, there are two. Special kapos rule like gods over the workers within the camp. There's an army of clerks. And so on.

Most doctors are toiling away as common workers. Only a few, thanks to personal connections, have managed to climb their way into the ranks of the big bosses. Their superior, Katz, the camp doctor, supposedly a dentist back home, receives us with the following little speech:

"Listen here, comrades! It seems I am the camp doctor. I'm not a bad guy, but for the record I must tell you that there are no patients here. If you can still move, you must go out to work. Even if you can't stand on your feet. Here no one is infirm and there is no medicine. And yet there is Bulldog, the SS medic, who flogs me if he finds more than ten people in the infirmary. And those ten can only be unconscious and dying, with a maximum of two hours of life left in them. Does anyone here have tobacco?"

We have no tobacco at the moment. Too bad, since, as later became clear, with its help confidential transactions could be made with the nicotine-obsessed dentist.

In fact, in this camp of six thousand, the SS officer nicknamed Bulldog allows only ten to fifteen "infirm" to be exempt from the daily deployment. Even though this Nazi naturally hasn't the slightest clue about the practice of medicine, he is the one who personally "examines" everyone who doesn't go to work, and he does so with thickheaded obstinacy. If he doesn't find them to be sick enough or Dr. Katz's assessment to be sufficiently persuasive, Bulldog then flogs the doctor and sends the patient packing with vigorous slaps. The hapless patient then seeks in despair to join up with the work unit nearest at hand, for woe unto him who is found in the camp during work hours without an assignment. That means death. The commander snoops around all day long within the barbed wire, and when he nabs a loafer he doesn't wait for the evening Appell to deal with him. He kicks him and canes him so thoroughly right then and there that the poor wretch rarely lives to see the next day.

That's the situation on the "health-care" front. Things aren't much different foodwise, either, though a huge kitchen is in operation. Completely unknown here is the so-called thick soup, or bunker soup, including extra carrots or potato peels in the warm water. We get milk soup rarely indeed, and even then without sugar. As for the sporadic potato dinners, those are subject to grievous tolls by the many hands they pass through along the way, from the Lagerälteste to Sanyi Róth, who doles out those dinners in Tent 28. Four or five rotten half-boiled potatoes comprise the Sunday menu.

After all this, here there is that special camp curse: the barter market. After the evening Appell, despite all our exhaustion, the camp transforms into a swarming beehive. The weary men jostle in the "market" by the gate. They sell and they buy. What? A smoker swaps his bread for a couple grams of bad makhorka tobacco or for a cigarette. Shrieking away, people offer muddy chunks of carrots, slices of fodder beets, onions, beets, heads of cabbage, potatoes, and even tomatoes. Rags and other stuff that can be used as handkerchiefs or suspenders; twine, dirty pages from a newspaper, for use in rolling cigarettes; handmade, primitive knives; spoons; empty cans. All manner of junk with trading value. Naturally, the wares are stolen. The sellers are from among the laborers at privileged workplaces: the vegetable farm that supplies the Tódt people, craftsmen's workshops, the castle interior the Pischl Company is rebuilding. Also on hand are quite a few resourceful men from work sites on the outskirts, who trade bread for tobacco from Ukrainians, and then later, back in the heart of the camp, sell that tobacco at a stiffly inflated price. Clever rascals make two Umans a day for themselves. An Uman is a filterless, rather stout Ukrainian cigarette. Several thin rods can be rolled from it, so it's held in high esteem even though its tobacco bites virulently at the throat.

Uman . . .

The name conjures up faint memories of things once read. The object of our desires, this nasty Ukrainian cigarette, bears the name of that Ukrainian city where in the middle of the eighteenth century, a massive massacre of Jews occurred—at least by the scale of those times. Around 1760, thousands of Jews were butchered.

The other type of cigarette is likewise Ukrainian. It has no brand. On account of its long, sheathlike filter, which takes up two-thirds of the cigarette's length, it is nicknamed Sheath. The exchange rate is one Uman to three Sheaths.

Sometimes "deals" are made even in makhorka, that quick-to-flare-up, nonaromatic tobacco dust, or in strong Hungarian tobacco. The hard currency: bread, soup, potatoes, margarine, and other extras. When a larger supply is available, tobacco can be had for various useful items as well. Naturally, the häftlinge buy not only tobacco, of which there is only sometimes enough to make it to the market, anyway. In exchange for bread or soup, the farm workers sell beets, kohlrabi, cabbage, and carrots.

We fall victim to an optical illusion. We are hard-pressed to resist the temptation of those colossal heads of cabbage. We can stuff one weighing maybe three kilos into ourselves for half a portion of bread—that's generally our thinking. The accounting naturally misses the most important factor: nutritional value.

Our rapid deterioration is no doubt accelerated by the barter market. Those with cabbages and beets, and nonsmokers, are often able to swap for themselves five or six lives' worth of bread, so they wind up eating more than do their comrades. Almost exclusively it's the calorie-rich bonuses that wander off to such clever traders.

This swapping frenzy is a heavy curse. Alongside our one thousand miseries, this is the one thousand and first. Those with tobacco soullessly plunder the ones longing for smoke. They form temporary cartels for the occasion and jack up the price. Sometimes they demand whole portions of bread for a pinch of makhorka tobacco.

Just before 9:00 PM the crowd disperses on the market square and private business ensues. Those who didn't manage to buy or sell at the market now go peddling door to door. The tents open up every minute. The emaciated, lice-infested bags of bones can hardly stand on their wounded, swollen feet, and yet they walk tirelessly about, parroting away in three or four languages:

"I'll give margarine for tobacco!"

"Cabbage for bread!"

"Mahorka for a rag towel!"

"I'll give potatoes for a Sheath!"

"Who has makhorka?"

"Kapo soup! Thick kapo soup!"

"*Schöne Suppe, schöne Suppe* [Lovely soup, lovely soup]*!*"

The seller shamelessly extols his product. Those interested rise from their pallets and, with rusty spoons, dip into the "thick kapo soup" to determine how much solid matter it contains. Then the desperate haggling begins. Those who don't understand each other's language communicate through gestures. The bread peddler passes a fingernail over a loaf to show how big a chunk he is willing to sell. The soup monger indicates a portion a few millimeters thicker. Buyer and seller shriek away in their mother tongues; curses fly about.

Bystanders scratch their heads while observing the battle seriously, thoughtfully. They too take a spoonful of the longed-for soup; they praise, they disparage, they advise. The whole thing is an agonizing give-and-take. There was a time when these people—those who now want nothing more than fewer lice, fewer beatings, and more swill, and pursue it with such self-abandon, desire concentrated in a single point of focus—would have given their dogs better food.

This, too, is the result of experimentation through scientific barbarism. Hundreds of thousands made to stand on all fours will no longer strive to vanquish the beast within themselves.

12

——

THE SITUATION IN 28 IS UNBEARABLE. IT SEEMS THAT Sanyi Róth hates me. He gives the paltriest bit of bonus food to me, always me, and I get the tiniest bit of bread. As for my place to lie down, it has been literally stolen. I'm lucky if I manage to squeeze between all those stinking bodies to pull through the night huddled up, thighs clenched. My bread has been stolen twice, though I placed it on the shelf above me just long enough to devour the soup. Proving such theft is impossible. The bandits do it with fiendish routine. They divvy up and gobble down the bounty in no time. Their reply to protest is masterfully coordinated feigned indignation.

Nor does poor little Bolgár fare any better. In an incautious moment, his undershirt and underpants vanished from the roof of 28, where he'd set them out to dry. By the time he raised a fuss, it was too late. Róth's chums had long "liberated them," and perhaps even sold them. They had gotten lucky: for three days they smoked. But they'd treated the kid badly. Little Bolgár's underwear had been in relatively good condition—a relic of our time in Eule, when he had worked for the Todts. He'd been concerned for his treasure and had guarded it jealously. Few people here, even among the big bosses, could boast of having underwear. Bolgár had spent hours patching it up on that one-third of each Sunday that was allotted to delousing and to washing our rags. Indeed, he'd gotten his hands on a needle, and strove tirelessly to exterminate the lice larvae from under the hems of the underpants.

To little Bolgár, this was a big blow. He wouldn't stop sulking. I had to do something. Things couldn't go on like this. One evening I got hold of Róth.

"Can I have a word with you, comrade?"

"What's it you want?"

"Why are you fellows picking on me and little Bolgár? We want to stay alive, too; to get home, if possible. What do you want from us?"

"You don't like it, huh?" he asks with a shrug. "Well, who invited you here, anyway?"

"You know we didn't ask to barge in here. If you guys don't make enough room for us to lie down, if you filch our grub and our rags, we'll drop dead. Don't you guys have any sense of camaraderie? Rogues once had hearts. Honor among thieves. I know, because I used to be a court reporter."

Róth's weather-beaten expression lights up.

"What the hell? You're a reporter? I thought you were some moronic business type."

"I *used to be* a reporter. As for Bolgár, he's a college student. His folks are superrich. Someday he might even be grateful. . . ."

"I don't give a damn about gratitude," Róth replies, knitting his brows. "Sanyi Róth never needed gratitude. You know who Sanyi Róth was in the underworld, anyway? Not since the great Vili Medvegy has there been a burglar like me."

Deep down, I rejoice. *Without intending to, I've wheedled my way to the soft spot of the burglar in him. Now he'll do all he can to convince me that he was the greatest. Sanyi Róth is entranced. It seems I was wrong: there is heart here, after all, perhaps even more than among those with clean records. Just a bit callused. So let's scratch off that callus!* Craftily I ask probing questions.

"How were you caught if you were such a class act? You guys came from the Kőhíd penitentiary, right?"

"You dope, surely you don't imagine they would have nabbed me just like that? My fence was caught, and the bastard ratted on me. I did forty-seven jobs, my man, and not a hair on my head was worse for it. I used to go to the horse races in Vienna in a sleeping car."

His tongue loosens. He softens, changed.

"Why didn't you say you're a reporter? I'll be telling you a story or two."

"That'll be good," I reply. "And from now on you'll leave us be."

"Not to worry. I'll talk to the boys."

With a knife he made himself, he cuts a big slice off the kohlrabi he's been chewing on the whole time.

"Take it. There will be more, too. My gig is at the Todt vegetable farm. I can bring some. And we'll have a chat every night."

I understood the symbolic significance of the gift. In this respect, little Bolgár and I could rest easy after this.

My conversation with Róth has an immediate effect. Without prompting, Misi, that park grifter and pickpocket whose face is white as flour and who looks like he has TB, moves aside with his blanket. I can finally stretch out. Jaksi, that servile fellow, begins addressing me as "Mister Editor" and offers me wood shavings. His associates likewise desist from the torment. The burglar commands unconditional respect in the tent. Not only do the lesser rogues respect the bigger rogue in him, but Róth also counts as a big boss of sorts. Though he has no title, he always has something with him. With superior skill he keeps drifting into the best work assignments, and at night he rarely shows up without "loot."

Bolgár's position is likewise reinforced under the protection of the room commander. He was born in a bubble, and once again luck is on his side. The little rascal has somehow wheedled his way close to the chief clerk, who is an engineer. He's been promised that he'll get to work in the Todt office here, too.

Within our quarters our woes fade away. But only there. The tunnel murders, and the weather has been retained as our executioner once and for all. It's raining nonstop. Even a half hour of sunshine is rare, as if it were December. And the camp commander makes his presence known with finely crafted brutalities. An SS sergeant, he is a gray-uniformed killer right off the assembly line, like his colleague at Eule, but more inventive at concocting tortures. No SS officer of higher rank is put in command of the lives and deaths of five or six thousand men. An ungainly peasant thirty to thirty-five years old, he has a remarkable accomplice in the weather. His favorite diversion is holding Appell in the rain.

Appell in the rain . . .

More tormenting than a whip, more murderous than a bullet.

The evening lineups last for hours, especially if it's raining. Our sergeant-henchman makes us stand about in a downpour for up to two hundred minutes. Meanwhile he is in the commandant's office picking at his nails or reading the Nazi Party newspaper, the *Völkischer Beobachter*, while puffing on his pipe. This is deliberate, perverse torture, annihilating agony of a special sort. Getting drenched and cold while hungry, full of lice, and black with rock dust—in water and mud, after stumbling about for thirteen hours. It's 11:00 PM by the time we're back in our unheated tents and we can cast off and wring out our sweaty, sodden garments. And then the next morning, at dawn, shivering and cursing, we throw the soaked rags back on ourselves. Is it a wonder, then, that after such diabolically inventive Appells rampaging pneumonia is the order of the day?

It is a perfected variation of this idea, which would befit the Inquisition, when all this happens on a Sunday, the day of rest. The rain then gets to soak us half the day.

The commandant has an imagination, and in the Lager-älteste and his fellow big bosses he finds those ready and willing to put his ideas into action. The aristocracy don't stand about with the rest of us. They can sprawl out in their tents, and only sometimes run the length of the rows, to check that the five-man columns are lined up properly.

As for lice, they are—in the literal, physical sense of the word—a burning matter. Our blankets are swarming with silvery-glistening colonies of larvae. Protecting ourselves is impossible: we've seen neither soap nor louse powder since we've been here, but barbers at the ready, mostly Greeks, precisely cut the prescribed "prisoner's band" across the thick layer of grime on our skulls once a week with dull, dirty clippers. Those in charge here do make sure of that, and only that.

The abominable vermin bring an end even to the relative calm of the nights. Everyone is scratching himself in awkward anguish while tossing and turning about in the stench of Tent 28. There's more room, though: by early September, five of us are dead.

There's a dysentery outbreak in the camp. Practically everyone comes down with the illness. Staying home is—naturally—impossible. With unconvincing words of encouragement, Dr. Katz and his assistants send all would-be patients packing after giving them two charcoal pills, as long as supplies last.

Fiery circles do a devil's dance before our eyes. We stagger about at the workplace in a stupor of weakness. Every couple of minutes we move over and squat, emptying pus. Bouts of diarrhea afflict some men twenty times a day. We experiment with "medications": We mix scorched pieces of wood into the infected water. We char potato skins. The kitchen staff does excellent business selling coffee-substitute dregs by the handful.

In the end, some recover and some die. After fifteen days of misery I am more or less back in order. I can't be more than forty kilos. My emaciated face is covered with a month of stubble; my bones are protruding; my knees, pointy. Not that there's a mirror anywhere, and it wouldn't make a bit of difference. Although we're together all the time, we can easily notice the frightening changes on each other from day to day.

To top it all off, a new horror emerges.

All at once the elongated faces become unnaturally rounded. Unprocessed fluid collects under the skin: on faces, bellies, arms, legs, everywhere. We bloat up. My knees and thighs swell. Every time I move, I pay for it with excruciating pain.

Our doctors shrug.

Hunger edema. The heart and the kidneys don't get through all that fluid without penalty. They can no longer handle it. We have to go out for roll call all the same. Bloated skeletons stand at Appell each morning at dawn.

The treatment would be simple: more substantial nourishment, less hot water in the guise of soup, and rest, rest, rest. . . . But all this is out of the question. In fact, every movement is a deadly risk to the overburdened heart. The daily death rate reaches unimaginable proportions. At work, corpses are simply dragged aside, and the robot-like labor goes on. The dead lie about for days until finally winding up in a lime pit.

Our SS guards start thinking: if this goes on, there will be a manpower shortage. Requesting new human cargo nowadays is difficult. The companies also take notice. Sänger und Lanninger doles out 250 grams of horsemeat to its men. All this helps precious little.

We stare at each other's faces, transformed into those of strangers. Death is spreading its wings over the cursed tent city. The gray ones act. As usual, they don't tackle the matter as they should: by improving our nourishment. Instead, for appearances, they come up with a new directive. Probably in the wake of a report filed by the camp commandant, so-called disinfection details appear and start fumigating the tents. A ludicrously futile measure. The lice obviously can't be exterminated with the häftling-disinfectors' primitive tools. At the moment, it's not as if that was the biggest problem, anyway.

János Vázsonyi is among the disinfectors. He arrived from Eule on a transport a few weeks after us. He and the others with him are housed a couple of kilometers away, in Camp 6.

He brings grievous news: Béla Maurer died in Eule. I turn away; my eyes are full of tears. I say a silent eulogy above this corpse that has surely been flung into the Eule cesspit, above the now motionless body of this man who'd loved to laugh and live, this man who'd been all heart:

You were wrong, after all, Béla. Your appraisal of the situation was off. How was it that you always put it? Lurking in every man is four months of reserve energy. And that it's a mathematical certainty that in four months this will be over. What month are we at now, Béla? I'm afraid it's October. Liberation has been late for six months already, and it's becoming more and more late. You did estimate the reserves well, though: you endured for around four months. You won't be writing that book anymore, my dear Béla, but you're right. One can drop dead from it, but one can't describe it at all. We suffer the ordeal and the indignity. . . . The living envy their dead. I envy you, Béla, my cheerful good friend. See how our manhood has prostituted itself. You must be happy, friend—you, who've already shaken off the chains of the senses—God be with you, au revoir. . . .

I'm involuntarily mumbling by the time I get to my closing words. We're standing about outside, eyes fixed to the ground, helpless. The sky no longer interests us: we stare at the earth, this cursed Teutonic earth, in whose parched, wretched soil the body of Béla Maurer, already half his onetime size, was now turning to dust. The tents are resounding with cries of woe and with curses, and before and behind us, like hopelessness closing in, the barbed wire stretches endlessly. It's October, Béla Maurer has died, and as for us . . .

"We don't have much longer to go," replies Vázsonyi quietly to the words I haven't spoken aloud.

His face, too, is unnaturally swollen, but it seems more balanced, calmer, I don't ask him how often he's tried suicide since then. I don't ask what remains of his moments of nicotine-fueled optimism.

He talks about Eule. The Feldmann plan naturally fell through immediately after the big relocations began. After our displacement, other transports were frequently sent on their way: in the area around Eule, it seems, less labor is needed, since construction is nearing completion.

I ask about news from the front. We are living here in a vacuum. Aside from this or that uncertain bit of information that's been through many hands before reaching us, we don't know anything.

"There's no problem there," he says. "The landing on the Western Front is going well, with events unfolding quickly. In the East, the Soviets are holding the initiative at all points. Hitler's armored divisions are in disorderly retreat. The Red Army is at the gates of East Prussia. The Romanians have pulled out. Budapest is being fenced in. The Arrow Cross are packing their bags."

He produces the torn-off front page of a German newspaper, the *Waldenburger Zeitung*. The three-column headline reads: "*Wachsender Druck der Feind gegen Budapest* [Increasing Enemy Pressure on Budapest]."

"Maybe, after all," I mumble on hearing that.

Staring into each other's puffed-up faces, we don't quite believe it.

Carefully putting away the shred of newspaper, he says earnestly:

"It's for cigarette paper—*if* I get my hands on tobacco. We have only thick sacks of cement in the camp. I haven't swallowed a gulp of smoke in three weeks, you know. Things are better where you guys are, as far as I can tell."

By chance I have a quarter pack of pipe tobacco on me. I bought it from an Italian for the special horsemeat from Sänger und Lanninger. Vázsonyi's face lights up. We pour the treasure carefully into the newsprint. *"Wachsender Druck der Feind . . ."*—that's what we twist it into.

We look at each other through a window of smoke. No, it's not so preposterous, after all. We'll go home. We'll buy tobacco at a tobacconist's. By the package. As much as we please . . .

* * *

Much, much later, after the liberation, on September 12, 1945, I read this in a Budapest daily:

"János Vázsonyi died yesterday in a German hospital."

13

A BIG EVENT OCCURS AT THE CAMP: "WINTER" CLOTHES
arrive. Trucks roll in loaded with assorted garb of woven
fabric. The stuff is carried to a separate barrack under the Lagerälteste's supervision. Our officers are busy all day long with
categorizing, selecting, and, well, ensuring the best items for
themselves and their minions.

Scraps from deportees' belongings: a hodgepodge of jackets,
trousers, and the like from civilian suits. The bulk and the best
of it has long ago been shipped off to the Third Reich: both the
front and the *Winterhilfswerk* (Winter Relief) donation drive need
warm stuff. As for our share, when it comes down to it—we
don't quibble during war—so what if someone at Birkenau had
taken off that pullover or fur coat? Each item has been meticulously dribbled with red and yellow paint. We'd already seen this
sort of thing from the train to Auschwitz.

I look forward hopefully to the change of clothing. It's time
to cast off my lice-infested rags.

Bitter disillusionment. I have no connections, and so all I
get is—a tunic. A bona fide tunic, with the buttons on the left.
Loose-fitting and thin at the same time, it doesn't help much. I
don't get pants.

And so I pull it over my old suit, and convince myself that I'm not so cold.

Toward the end of October, fall strikes and then unfolds right on schedule. I'm in worse shape with each passing day. I don't even notice; Sanyi Róth does. Over the course of these weeks it turns out that he's quite a decent fellow, especially when a good dose of vanity—having to do with his professional achievements—is stirring in him. Out of gratitude for the steadfast patience with which I listened to tales of his glory days as a burglar, in his own way he now takes me once and for all under his protection. He regularly gives me beets and cabbage, though he isn't even working anymore at the kitchen of the Todts. Sometimes he even adds a cigarette butt. All this is quite something, a seriously good deed. The burglar always finds a way. He gobbles down twice as much as others, invariably drifts to a new work unit, and regularly "liberates" some sort of food or an item of value that can be exchanged for it.

"You'll be finished in two weeks," he concludes decisively and with not much tact. "Why don't you try to get away from Sänger?"

"But how?"

"Ah, my boy, they don't teach this in school. You've got to figure out something."

My situation has become even more dire in the past two weeks, as I've wound up on the night shift. We work nonstop from 8:00 PM to 6:00 AM. This is the hardest, most hated job. The nighttime kapos are one degree more bloodthirsty, while the foremen and the Italian skilled workers are more brutal. Constant rockfalls threaten to crush us every second of the endless night. The drills' blaring roar all but makes us deaf, and my swollen knees respond to every move with unbearable pain.

The *Nachtschicht*—night shift—workers sleep by day. During the day only those assigned to work within the camp, the Älteste, the clerk, the officers, and, indeed, the hooligan commandant stay behind in the camp, which is otherwise rather deserted. Sanyi Róth's ominous warning leads me to resolve to venture over to the clerk and ask him to intercede.

Let's give it a try. I step over to him, and—the very thought is absurd—begin by introducing myself. Not with a number, but a name. In my experience—from long ago and far away—you can set the tone at will of a first conversation with a stranger. If I introduce myself, maybe he'll involuntarily tell me his name, too. He will subconsciously set the tone. And kicks generally do not follow an introduction.

Besides, that first clerk doesn't promise to be such a bad option. One time I noticed him spooning milk soup for himself on the bench in front of his tent. A small group of hungry häftlinge were gaping at the spectacle, naturally from a respectful distance. The clerk—perhaps his palate sensed the silent pleading—waved a hand at random at one of them to come over, and without a word he poured what was left into the häftling's tin can.

"Forgive me for disturbing you, Mr. Engineer, sir, I have a vital request for . . ." I know he'd been an engineer somewhere in Czechoslovakia.

So I begin, introducing myself by name, prompting him to say his name, too, which the whole camp already knows and dreads.

Caught off guard by the unusual situation, this man—who's

grown attached to his rubber truncheon and turned more vicious from all the commands he barks—casts me a nonplussed glance.

"Go ahead," he says. I show him my swollen leg and ask him to move me to a different work unit. *If I need to stay longer in the tunnels*, I think, *I'm done for.*

"What's your number?"

"33031."

He jots it down. It's called out at the Appell early the next morning.

The result is quick: I'm assigned to the Pischl Company, which is in charge of rebuilding the castle itself. From that day forward, my work sites change often. One day I'm shoveling sand onto a conveyor belt, carrying gravel, or filling a cement mixer. The next day, I am lugging this and that in a forest of metal beams to the point where my ligaments are tearing. Along with my companions, I press hard against rail carts filled to the brim with lumps of earth and against excruciatingly heavy "Japans," or iron boxcars.

Our company kapo is Max, who'd been Lagerälteste—Camp Elder—in Eule. He managed to wheedle his way into this new position, and now, his glory having faded, he seeks to validate his tattered dignity.

At least it's a big plus that I am working aboveground. Sky is now falling on me from overhead, not rocks. I drink in the brightness, devour the stingy sun. A powerful resolve matures in me: I want to live, to live again.... I make a vow: no longer will I buy more tobacco in exchange for food. I want to live; I want to go home.... To run amok taking revenge, calling to account, and meting out justice to those who dragged me here.

I become inventive. The furious desire to live makes me so. I too undertake little ventures. I begin sneaking into the castle, where only the most privileged are employed, those engaged in interior work. I start pilfering. I make off with everything that finds its way into my hands and that I can hide, unnoticed, under my loose-fitting tunic. A shabby old shoe brush, a piece of sackcloth, paper, a tin can—every little something that has trading value—off it goes with me into the camp. People buy electric cables to use as belts, rags for foot cloths. On one occasion I manage to "liberate" several bags' worth of paper wadding. Among those bleeding from a thousand wounds, this is a veritable treasure, and I fare extraordinarily well selling it.

The tiny thefts naturally come with deadly risk. If I am ever caught, I won't survive the accusation. But I'm not caught. Indeed, almost every day I get hold of a pinch of makhorka, and sometimes I can even trade cabbage or beets.

I want to go home. . . .

Every night after soup distribution, the kettles are returned by the men of a different tent to the kitchen barracks beyond the barbed wire. It sometimes happens that I formulate a meticulous plan for the day when Tent 28 has its turn to carry the kettles. In front of the kitchen are piles of potatoes and kohlrabi. There I pretend to trip, cleverly falling flat on my belly, right in the middle of the mountain of treasure, and as I stagger back onto my feet, cursing away, more than a few precious potatoes vanish into my tunic's voluminous pockets.

I'm proud that not even the experts among my tentmates notice my little scheme. Sanyi Róth would surely praise me if I let him in on it.

At the end of the day, though, every last bit of the will to live is inevitably drowned in the hellish vortex we inhabit. The mills of God grind slowly—those of the death camps, faster. The ash of this bitter recognition quickly extinguishes the flame of hope that burns in more tranquil moments. All around me are examples of reality: lice larvae, bunker soup, corpses flung on the trash heap, swollen living dead, rubber truncheons, and revolvers. Days of despondency, of lethargy, then come again, those days from which I had once roused myself.

Dysentery takes hold of me yet again. Swelling spreads frighteningly over my entire body. Over the course of these days I am lugging sacks of cement to the mixers, and I become hopelessly dirty. The cement dust swirling nonstop in the air forms a thick layer of sediment upon my clean-shaven head. It collects on my gums and seeps into my nose, my eyes, my ears. Not even Sanyi Róth can get his hands on soap. I hang my rags on the nail above me. The pants and the tunic are literally moving from the thousands of squirming lice. Destroying them is hopeless to begin with, so lately we haven't even been trying.

So it is that a big day comes: November 13. Around 3:00 AM the door of Number 28 is kicked open. The light of handlamps shines upon those at rest.

"*Achtung* [Attention]*!*"

We all spring to our feet mechanically, half-asleep. The camp commandant. Behind him, Bulldog, the SS medic, Camp Doctor Katz, the two Lagerältesten, and the chief clerk. Katz is holding a slip of paper in his hand. They stop by the entrance.

The commandant turns to Katz:

"*Also los! Nur rasch!* [Let's go! Be quick!]*"*

"Boys!" the doctor sputters—his hand lamp lighting up his waxy yellow face—"I've got a somber task. I can't talk much: this wild beast hardly wanted to let me even speak in Hungarian in the Hungarian tents. In short: what this is about is that I've got to pick out four hundred people. Those will be on their way at dawn. Where to, no one knows for sure at the moment. I don't want to mislead anyone, so I'll be frank: unofficial reports are that Birkenau is the destination. At least that's what the commandant thinks. You know the rest. . . ."

He chokes up, stammering:

"I . . . I . . . have already said all this thirty-four times this evening. . . . I'm not a murderer; I'm not a mass murderer. . . . That's not what I want to be. . . . I can't take it. . . . I don't know what to say. . . . God damn the bastards. . . . This is terrible."

He looks us over imploringly.

"Will someone volunteer?"

Comprehending what's just been said is hard. We stare, petrified, at the gray ones stomping impatiently about and at the three häftlinge, the spine-chilling moment having flayed off their rough-edged haughtiness. They too are slaves, like us. Tomorrow it could be their turn.

"*Also, was ist den los* [So, what's going on]?" The commander is losing his patience as well. They still have to visit many tents.

Katz glances at the list.

"Hurry up, boys! No one? Then I've got to—"

"You don't. I'll drop dead in the end, anyway. Two weeks earlier or later, it's all the same."

Misi, the pickpocket.

"Your number?"

"72154."

"Next? We need four men from every tent. Quickly now!"

"76525."

One-eyed Pereldik. Rumor has it that he was a cat burglar until he was caught.

"Hell with it all," he says. "The hole we're off to will have as many comforts as this joint."

Little Bolgár casts me a questioning look. I nod.

"37608," comes the kid's trembling voice.

"33031," I quickly add.

Katz sighs with relief.

"That's enough. Just don't lose your spirit. It's not certain, after all. The one thing that's for sure is that you'll be leaving from here by dawn. In the end it almost doesn't matter"—he adds quickly—"since sooner or later every one of us will go off the deep end, anyway."

He continues in German:

"Those whose numbers I've written will not lie back down but will go at once to the barber barracks. And then line up in front of the infirmary."

Gesticulating with his revolver, the commandant now speaks:

"Wash thoroughly. Any Jew whose head on which I find dirt..."

With menacing emphasis, he falls silent. He then turns to Katz:

"*Fertig* [Ready]?"

"*Jawohl, Herr Kommandant* [Yes sir, Commandant]."

"*Also weiter* [So, on]."

They leave noisily. No one in 28 will go back to sleep on this night.

"Have you guys gone crazy?" Róth barks at us, but his voice is uncertain. "Maybe he wouldn't have chosen you? All of us here are pretty much dead meat."

"Look, Sanyi," says little Bolgár, now calmly scratching himself while getting ready. "I, for example, have been wanting for months to do myself in. One day you suddenly imagine death to be like some sumptuous, refreshing steam bath. If I'd had the courage, I would have already done something a long time ago. Now I've cast off the problem. Let them tighten the noose."

"As for myself," says Misi, getting to his feet, "for half a year now I haven't been full, haven't had a clean change of clothes. What's awaiting me? Not even liberation excites me. We've hit the jackpot, I swear."

Pereldik steps out front by the door without a word. He takes a whiff of the cold November night. I too am silently getting ready. Of the four of us, I'm the only one with a little pack of belongings. The product of my recent zeal. I've kept the stuff in a tattered package that once held biscuits: a piece of dirty cotton, a couple of rags, and sheets of newspaper. Aside from a rusty spoon and a tin can, I too have nothing else.

The others surround us with curious sympathy. Waves of goodness seize them on seeing the four of us headed toward presumed death. Róth bids farewell by handing me a bit of cabbage and a good-size Uman cigarette stub. In the minds of those staying behind, this imperative throbs away: *We've got to give, to give something.* They see halos above our lice-infested heads, halos imbued with the somber majesty of death by gas.

And yet a few of us are to meet again in the cold crematorium of the camps. But who could have known this now? Everyone—we and our comrades alike—was convinced that Birkenau's conveyor belt awaited those about to depart. The words Katz had thrown at us—"not certain"—struck us as cold comfort, feeble encouragement.

In the barber barracks, those set to leave are wailing, with the Greeks among us creating a panicked uproar. Their delirious lamentation makes me shudder and shakes my resolve.

But after two hours, once the four hundred of us line up, I'm calm again; shivering, but now only from the cold. Never would I have thought it possible to come to terms so completely with the thought of dying, nay, that the thought of imminent death should become outright desirable.

We have to remove the smooth-fabric clothes we got recently. When the trucks arrive, our purple-hued, puffed-up bodies are once again covered by coarse rags.

Not by train or by foot—but by truck. Rarely does the comfort of a motor vehicle mean life in the Land of Auschwitz. Our commandant follows through on his nighttime threat by caning us diligently. Duty comes first. . . . He'd rather sacrifice the few hours of night that remain than shirk his duty. We're not clean enough. Just how we would have conjured ourselves into that condition he forgets to enlighten us.

Now, too, we get two days' worth of bread and margarine. They squeeze eighty of us into each truck.

It must be around 4:00 AM. Moonlight accompanies us, bright and cold. As do machine-pistol-toting guards. By now we're not so chilly: squeezed in tight, we warm each other. I wolf down my bread, bite off some margarine to go with it, and wear away my teeth on Sanyi Róth's cabbage.

Huddled beside me is little Bolgár. Twilight shimmers on a teardrop sprouting on his face.

14

—

IN THE LATE AFTERNOON WE MAKE A TURN AND FIND OURSELVES behind barbed wire. Slender chimneys stand guard behind a long, ramshackle stone building.

Chimneys—as anticipated, but the building itself is more reminiscent of a sort of factory than a crematorium. What's certain is that we're not in Birkenau, but what good is that? East and west, north and south, the empire of camps is flanked by Birkenaus small and large.

The two-story structure seems abandoned. Its chimneys are not billowing smoke; the only smoke to be seen—thin bands shooting skyward—is from the chimneys of the rows of green barracks deep in the spacious yard. On hearing the drone of our trucks' engines, a single häftling slowly emerges from the center door of the main building.

"Where are we?" a hundred mouths cry out.

A smile of sorts slinks across the native's apathetic expression. He replies in Yiddish:

"Don't let the chimneys scare you. It's not a crematorium."

"And?"

"Dörnhau, camp hospital. Haven't you heard about us?"

A cacophony of voices. Of course. We'd heard that there were so-called hospital camps, but that was all we knew.

So the sympathy that had embraced us back in Fürstenstein had been wasted on nothing. I'm chewing Sanyi Róth's farewell cabbage, but undeservedly. Now what would Number 28 say to this turn of events?

"What's the situation here?" That's the first thing we want to know.

The häftling—who, it later turns out, is a bigwig, one of the clerks at Dörnhau—suddenly stiffens. Fraternizing is incompatible with his job.

"Don't ask so many questions! Shut your traps and line up!"

We're handed over to others, and already we're headed inside.

There are huge rooms one above the other on the first, second, and third floors. A factory's abandoned, dismantled engine rooms. They now contain long rows of bunk beds. Two or even three half- or completely naked men occupy each bunk—whether stretched out, sitting, huddled, squeezed tight against each other, or standing. Only a few have blankets.

No tranquility here, that's for sure.

The November cold pours in through the broken windows, and yet the stench is unbearable all the same. A suffocating stink oozes from the walls. Rising between the rows of bunks, several centimeters high, is an odious yellowish slurry of dung. Naked skeletons are sloshing through the putrid river.

First impression: We've wound up among raving maniacs. A dizzying cacophony of moaning, whimpering, shrieking, whining, and delirious snarling. The underworld is seething.

All at once, at least twenty men scream:

"Pot! Pot!"

The "pot" is a dented tin bucket into which those who can't get up relieve themselves—assuming it reaches them in time. Those who carry the pots are usually deaf to the wailing cries urging them to come. The bucket nearly always arrives late, and the bedridden person either soils himself or, more often, does his business on the floor. Everyone has diarrhea. Hence the horrid yellow streams along the rows of beds.

Every bucket carrier is cursing, hitting, and snarling. He and the person demanding it engage in ceaseless hand-to-hand combat. At first I don't understand how someone could take on such a revolting task. Later I learn that the carriers themselves are sick. It's for a larger chunk of bread that such a patient-worker stumbles about from morning to night in the sea of human sludge.

Not even an hour goes by, and I'm no longer able to take pleasure in the fact that this isn't Birkenau. Later, amid the torments of the cold crematorium, I will be often haunted by the specter of those first minutes in Dörnhau, conjuring up the images that greeted me. It took time getting used to, but once initiated among the screaming, naked, wild men, I too was one of them.

Cold crematorium . . .

I first hear this apt designation from Dr. Haarpruder when he walks by the new arrivals. At one time Dr. Haarpruder was a well-regarded heart specialist in Transylvania or Bihar. Here he is not exactly an illustrious figure in the populous hierarchy of doctors.

Dörnhau has a labyrinthine and pathologically sprawling camp aristocracy. There must be five thousand people in the

cold crematorium when we arrive. Of those, at least five hundred
have some sort of office, and they play the tyrant accordingly.
The prestigious branch of this nobility is the corps of sixty to
seventy doctors. At its helm is the chief physician, Dr. Párdány,
from Upper Hungary, who is one of the foremost powers in the
camp's big hospital. Dr. Haarpruder is a junior officer in the
group that Dr. Párdány heads. Párdány's lieutenants and aides:
gruff, fat Dr. Auer; Grau, that amateur surgeon, who does am-
putations on a rough wooden table using a carpentry saw, with
predictable "results." Completing the roster are Dr. Warschauer
and Dr. Erzberger, a dentist specializing in gold teeth.

The corpse bearers must account to Erzberger for what they
pry out. He then hands over the illicit profit to the Lagerälteste,
who turns over most of it to the camp commandant and the
German chief medic, with the remainder divvied up among the
top brass, in brotherly fashion. By the time we arrived, according
to rough estimates, more than twenty kilos of gold had already
been distributed this way.

Everyone knows this, and everyone considers it natural. It's
become widespread practice for even the living to sell the treasures lurking in their oral cavities. A whole army of häftlinge
has come to specialize in extracting gold for modest compensation from the mouths of those who volunteer. It's mainly the
kitchen workers who buy such gold, in exchange for soup. One
gold crown yields special soup every day for a week. That's the
going rate.

Párdány and those around him lead the army of doctors. Naturally, even doctors of lower rank are privileged. However, by no
means does the caste accept all the newly arrived doctors, who

by now are, for all intents and purposes, not officers but privates: outpatients and inpatients, common workers. There are, indeed, a hundred doctors and medical students stuck outside of Eden.

The other branch of the camp aristocracy is the noble order of the medics. Most of them reach the pot of lard owing to family ties or friendships, their original occupations having nothing to do with caring for the sick. Their ruler is a lawyer called Miklós Nagy. It's said that he had two thousand acres back home. He is an antsy, lanky young man of the sort who compensates for his physical slightness with bluster that has transformed itself here into sadism. He hasn't been sane for a long time. In fact, he is outright mad, but he is in charge. His specialty: striking the soles of bare feet and doing Indian war dances on the victim's naked belly. I once saw this lightweight man jump up and down on a patient's chest like a rubber ball, stomping on him with bloodshot eyes until he was worn out. The victim's crime: he'd tried conniving his way to a second helping of soup.

The head medic gentleman is surrounded by lieutenants. Every rooster is king of his own trash heap, and this is certainly apt here: each lieutenant was the absolute ruler of his dump. The block medic rules over a block together with the Blockälteste. Each big hall, one above the other on the three floors, comprises a separate block. Aside from this, there are many sickrooms small and large in every corner of the building. These, too, are divided into blocks. With the exception of the bosses' smaller, more comfortable rooms, every space in the factory is filled with bunks.

A so-called healthy division some two hundred strong occupies the middle floor. Its residents go to work every day. Together with the prisoners of the neighboring Kaltwasser camp, they are building the Nazis' underground state.

On every floor, the immediate commander of each row of bunks is the group medic, with two deputies, backed up by an army of soup carriers, bread distributors, sweepers, bucket carriers, and those who undress and carry corpses. The latter come from among the *Schonung*, prisoners, those deemed unfit for regular work. Every such group oversees 100 to 150 of the bedridden. Their most immediate almighty gods are the group medic and his deputies.

The hierarchy of doctors and that of other health-care staff comprise two of the camp's sky-high rank ladders. A third, lush branch is the army of locusts with Lagerälteste Muky Grosz at the helm: Ältesten; corpse kapos; *Revier* kapos, those in charge of the barracks housing sick prisoners; and clerks. While Muky sounds like a nickname denoting affection, trust, or intimacy, that wasn't at all the case here. This is how the Lagerälteste signs his name on the orders he posts on the walls of the blocks.

There's also a fourth category of the privileged: the kitchen workers. Cooks, helpers, bread slicers, boiler cleaners, potato peelers. Kapos and commoners.

All these titles, ranks, and roles are certainly not meaningless terms. Each carries real power. On the one hand, on account of the privileged workplace and proximity to the soup kettle, it means more, and more varied, food. This power is also manifested in wanton despotism—issuing commands, meting out punishments, and committing sundry brutalities. An officeholder can flog you, kick you to death, deprive you of food; he can exploit or terrorize you as he well pleases.

Shining above them all are the two rarely seen sovereigns: the

Lagerälteste and the chief doctor. Both are outcasts, as are the rest of us, but amid misfortune fortune has taken them into its arms.

When they appear with their entourage in the block, the word "Attention" blares out just the same as if it were a gray one arriving. A tragicomic scene. The prisoner in a striped uniform, his lieutenants trailing humbly behind him, stepping along the rows of bunks issuing commands and punishments. With no more than a glance of his eyes or wave of a hand, Muky—that short-statured clerk from Bratislava with an angular jaw—smites lightning and doles out mercy; he lifts people up and drops them down. Compared to him, Max, from Eule, and Berkovits, from Fürstenstein, are modest authority figures.

Our SS guards live separately, in the small office building. They show themselves rarely: everything happens through and by the will of our häftling slave drivers. The lives and deaths of six thousand people, the anguish they suffer and what relief they may experience, depend on the two camp kings.

For three days now I've been in Block A, on the ground floor. No one has lifted a finger to ensure us spots in the crowded bunks. Each of us must struggle to do so on his own. Squeezing in while naked monsters are kicking away in protest and cursing furiously isn't easy, but it works.

As it happens, I get a bunk of my own. I'm in luck: I'm able to pounce on a bottom bunk toward the end of the first street, across from one of the food-distribution stalls. Two corpse bearers have just lifted a naked body off it. The blanket is still on the bed, its folds still revealing the contours of the freshly removed corpse. The lair is still steaming with the heat of the cadaver, which hadn't even cooled off. But I'm not being squeamish; barely anyone among us is still capable of being disgusted.

I'm naked, like the others. My rags were taken away. According to Dr. Haarpruder, the bedridden don't need clothing; every last garment is needed by those able to walk.

Shivering, I hide under the blanket, which moments ago had been covering an unknown, dead comrade. I think of Birkenau, which, lo and behold, was not my destiny, after all.

For now, everything seems implausible. It's hard to awaken from the delirious specter, to rise out of the numbing terror everyone sinks into on stepping into this place. I simply don't believe my eyes. I decide that frightening visions have entrenched themselves in my agitated self. I pull the dead man's lice-infested blanket over my head and stay there for hours. I seek light in the darkness, conjuring up a lost reality behind my closed eyelids.

I am burning in the cold crematorium.

15

I'M NOT ALONE FOR LONG IN MY BUNK. PEOPLE ARE RARELY left at peace in Block A. The deranged machinery of the place is set to constant motion. Transfers between blocks, bunk changes, the chaos of soup distribution, scheduled delousing, officious inspections and canings, the handing out of food coupons, and the removal of dead bodies—all this happens one after the other.

A couple of hours after I laid my claim to my place in the bunk, a neighbor is pushed in beside me. An unconscious old man, eyes shut. His shrunken face is lost beneath the thick layer of dirt; lice are stirring on his unkempt gray mustache. His bloodless lips sometimes emit groaning sighs. He is raving in Yiddish. Never have I noticed such deep and tragic resonance in that language, which invariably sounds a bit comic to a Jew for whom, like me, Hungarian is his mother tongue.

I stare at my neighbor, the dying old man. What the outside world would whisper—*sympathy*—still resonates in me: I arrived just three days ago. The others—the naked people squeezed in beside us and between us—aren't bothered by his agony one bit.

To say it's crowded around here is an understatement. On average, five people are lying on each narrow bunk, and yet others are placed by the feet of those already there and over them. Transports small and large are arriving nonstop from various camps. Apparently by an order from on high, it's here that those in the worst condition are being collected. There's a dying man in nearly every other bunk.

With a blanket I cover the old man's grimy thighs, which look like a child's arms, and I lean over him. The man opens his stubborn brown old eyes, revealing unnaturally dilated pupils and bloodshot eyeballs.

"Water," he moans. "Give me some water, you damn bastards. . . . Sarah! . . . Sarah! . . . Help! . . . Sarah, you stinking bitch, why don't . . . you come . . . already. . . . Water! . . ."

His voice dies out; his eyes close.

I turn to the bunk to my left:

"We need to get some water."

"Just leave it be. He'll be done for in a half hour, anyway." So advises Miksa Rosenfeld from beside me. A grizzled, fiftyish tough guy, he is the loudest bigmouth in the neighborhood. The slimy fellow is smeared with all kinds of fat. Figuratively speaking, of course. None of us has seen any fat in weeks.

This Rosenfeld is constantly planning, speculating, offering trades for the next soup rations, and picking fights with the person handing out bread. What will be today's bonus? Artificial honey or jam?

Not even he can get up, and like most everyone else here, he is able to use only a bucket, but he speaks of home in such a way and with such self-assurance that it's as if he left the day before yesterday and is returning the day after tomorrow. You've got to be really careful around him, and it's advisable to wolf down your ration right away, since Rosenfeld is a whiz at thievery. He is as crafty as a Greek, and his well-feigned indignation when caught disarms even the person who has been wronged.

Now that I'm troubling myself over the dying old man, Rosenfeld tries with apparent benevolence to talk me out of it.

"The water is contaminated, anyway—drinking it is prohibited. If one of the bigwigs sees it, that's bad trouble."

Ignoring him, I look around for water. As a newcomer, I don't yet have a can. The one I'd brought from Fürstenstein was stolen the first day.

"Give me your can," I snap at him. "I'm getting water."

"Hell with that!"

Indeed, it takes a good dose of naïveté to assume that someone would hand over the container he can't do without, much less let it wander beyond his eyeshot.

I give in. I must admit that wanting to help is hopeless. That's when I feel moist warmth under me. Repulsed, I rise to my knees. The dying man's excrement is slowly spreading out on the bunk's wood shavings.

I become hysterical and begin shouting. Everyone around me laughs.

"You're still squeamish, comrade," comes a voice from the bunk across from me. "But you'll get over it." It's Israel, whose face and entire body are covered with terrible, open sores. "Seems the old man has had it. Most folks soil themselves at the final moment. That's their farewell from the world."

Rosenfeld rises, and leans over the body.

"He's dead," he says, and then turns anxiously to the neighborhood. His voice is half-commanding, half-questioning:

"Should we sit him up?!"

Intense deliberations ensue. Bargaining, assigning of roles. How to sit him up needs to be arranged.

This is an everyday trick: only those who have the strength to sit up when food is handed out get soup and bread. Those who remain lying down in major moments—so goes the Lager-älteste's outlandish claim—are necessarily dead, or, at least, dying. And the dead and the dying don't need food. The bosses pick up the daily provisions based on the morning head count, and divvy up what's left, and that's substantial.

The bedridden are contriving shrewdly. It's pitch-black as the evening distribution unfolds. The supervisor of those delivering the food is the only person with a light in his hand, a glass-enclosed candle stub. The neighborhood ad hoc interest group sits up the dead and the dying. They adjust stiff hands into stretched-out poses, while, unnoticed, living hands behind them seize upon the food handed out all along the rows. After some bickering, the organizers split the bounty. The weak then battle it out over spoonfuls of vile liquid. Tumbling over the bellies of the dead, they snatch bread from each other's hands.

The medics record the previous day's dead the next morning, and it's usually noon by the time the actual removal of bodies occurs. The touch of the ever-colder body pressed tight up against me fills me with revulsion. I can't help but wonder at how calmly our mutual neighbor, Weisz, the stuttering barber from Košice, puts his feet on the belly of the corpse.

Strangely enough, the lethargy that spreads over the eyes and the brain, the semiconscious numbness, helps. What's real doesn't register. Again, I turn to the reality behind shut eyes, as on my arrival, kindling memories from the life outside. I do so even as my head and feet are butting up against steaming bodies, even as my waterlogged body responds with pain to every touch, and even as those around me are cursing and wailing away in Hungarian, Polish, and Yiddish.

The stall that serves as a food storeroom closes late at night. Specially appointed prisoners considered unfit for regular labor stand guard over it all night long. Our commanders withdraw, and eventually even the barter market in front of the hallway leading to the latrine empties out. Shivering away, the nighttime bucket carriers take up their posts by the block medic's fenced-off enclosure. Those able to do so get off their bunks and join the procession of naked men dragging their feet to the latrine. An icy wind howls in through the broken window.

Our steaming bodies don't alleviate the cold, nor is the wind a match for the vile odor of this pigsty, a stench that has already permeated people, stone, and wood. Everything, ineradicably, as with the lice.

Night falls heavily in Dörnhau.

We've chewed up the bread and polished off the soup. Even those who don't have an hour of life left in them have lapped it all up. The diarrhea stricken, who can no longer eat solid food, slip their bread with trembling hands under the wood shavings of their bunks.

In Dörnhau, those whose turn has come depart mostly after dark. The nights belong to struggling moans, screaming fare-wells, and delirious wails for home.

Come here, you visionaries who create with pen, chalk, stone, or paintbrush; all of you who've ever sought to conjure up the grimace of suffering and death; prophets of the *danse macabre*, engravers of terror, scribes of hells—come here!

Night in Dörnhau.

Six hundred men are pressed tightly up against each other. Every third one is writhing, whimpering, groaning, gurgling, raving. Every third person is dying.

Some are whining for doctors deliriously, stubbornly—more to themselves than to anyone else. The thin tailor above me thinks he is at home, talking to his little boy. By tomorrow, he won't be around, knitting caps in exchange for soup from well-heeled bigwigs.

Above me, under me, all around me, this army of people ready to depart is crying out for God and water. Eyes turning glassy are soaking in the darkness of Hades or the foolish pinkness of heaven. Death is stepping between the bunks like a learned, confident young professor feeling quite at home.

The wailing is contagious. Like dogs howling at the moon, all six hundred of us are aimlessly whining away. A choir of raving flagellants.

The icy granary with the broken windows resounds with eerie voices and shrieks of despair, horror, and fear.

This concert of outcasts lasts until the wee hours of the morning, when the first gray filters in. Then, silence. Without warning, without reason, just as the uproar started earlier.

Two hundred die in one block that night.

As daybreak takes hold, the bunks fall silent. The dead and the living alike doze off.

A hustle and bustle ensues at 5:00 AM: the wake-up call for the work detail on the fourth floor. Before the Appell they assemble here, in Block A. This is the way to the latrine. This time it's a different sort of racket that rouses the hall, but no longer a bothersome one. The bedridden in Block A may be motionless, but few are asleep. The workers are now being given their bread ration—four times as much as we get. Tracked by covetous eyes, the thriftier among us are now chewing on pieces of bread saved earlier. The stirring spectacle rips open hunger's wounds. We try getting back to sleep; sleep wins us time. One loaf of bread is divided into eleven pieces. A few of us succeed at our desperate struggle toward dreams, but at nine all must finally wake up in any case. Medics are going up and down the bunk streets, calling out, in both Hungarian and German:

"Halottakat bejelenteni! Toten anmelden! [Report the dead!]"

The more jocular among us come up with a variation: "Report if you're dead!"

Reporting is always the responsibility of the immediate neighbors. The medics jot down the number of the dead and of the bunk. The commander of the corpse-bearing detail then shows up with his two men, who are carrying a makeshift stretcher made of wooden boards. With the help of the neighbors, they grab the corpse and unceremoniously heave it into the river of dung. They tie a small tag to a big toe with the former häftling's number and are already off with the body. For now, the neighbors rejoice over the better, bigger space on the bunk, the momentary cessation of the discomfort caused by the corpse. After all, they can't procure his bread ration for today, seeing as how the death has been registered and the man's share removed from the list.

As for the one who's moved on, he continues his fleeting journey in the corpse barracks. From here he ends up in the common lime pit dug beside the camp. Before that, his gold teeth are wrenched out. The naked witnesses of the Dörnhau night become the dust of this cursed German land. They have no names, just numbers, and even that is ensured for only a few weeks or months of immortality by the camp clerk's tattered, death-registration notebook.

The neighbors' relief doesn't last long. After 9:00 AM, new shipments pull into the cold crematorium one after another by foot, car, or truck.

16

O UR BLOCK MEDIC IS CALLED JUDOVICS. THIS DESPOT OF
Block A is around twenty-one years old. I became an involuntary witness to his meteoric rise. Starting out as a soup
carrier, with trickery he ensured himself extra helpings of food.
Once done with his shift, sprawled out on his bunk, he takes
pleasure in methodically chewing away what he's stolen. He can
be bribed: for half a bonus ration he'll conjure extra soup out
of the kettle. The business has taken off, and Judovics has fast
become a tycoon. The bigwigs have taken note of his brutality, his soulless airs, his sycophantic yelling, and, not least, his
exceptional physical condition. Soon he was appointed bread
supervisor. When Block A's medic and pharmacist, the despised
Steinfeld, was promoted to the position of Revier kapo—
infirmary kapo—Judovics succeeded him as the one sitting on
the block's neck.

This shady, stammering brat had been among those who, in
his earlier life, had "not amounted to anything." He couldn't
even write his name, and back home he'd been constantly battling it out with the justice system. But now, in the swamp of
the death factory, he truly blossomed. Tyranny and cruelty were
right up his alley. Being quite the schemer, he knew just how

to make himself indispensable to those at the top, who didn't much bother with Block A. After all, this ground-floor hall was gradually becoming the death row for those nearing the end. All those branded incurable after the usual superficial examination were thrown in here. Most of those could no longer stand on their two feet. They'd become so weak that their flaccid, atrophic leg muscles couldn't bear even the weight of their now shriveled, skeletal torsos. When a häftling in this condition sometimes tried getting up to go relieve himself, he could immediately collapse like a rag doll.

It is under Judovics's supervision that the block receives its bread, bonuses, and kettles of soup. He oversees the distribution.

Every day, we await 11:00 AM and 8:00 PM with trembling. All eyes are anxiously anticipating the arrival of the decisive moment, and those still able to get up prepare themselves for the great ritual: eating. The skeleton-people greedily clutch the iron spoons they've pulled out from under the wood shavings. Soup is being delivered to the bunks. As the food carriers approach, excitement mounts: restlessly we observe their every motion through the sludge, and pick apart the news that flits from bunk to bunk:

"Bunker soup," comes a report from the end of the row.

Apprehensively a question flits right back:

"Thin?"

"Hot water."

And yet we attend to it voraciously. First we dip in our spoons to determine if carrots, beets, potato skins, or other bunker soup ingredients are swimming about deep inside. The lucky ones get a thicker portion, and the carriers have put aside better soup for those with good connections. In exchange for thicker liquid, wheeler-dealers immediately hand over half their margarine or their sticky chunk of congealed artificial honey to Judovics and his henchman, who go about their business with lofty airs.

Judovics is the conductor of such major moments. His eyes are everywhere, and he harshly punishes cheating of all sorts, for such doings ultimately mean less for him, the great swindler. When catching someone red-handed in the act of sitting up a corpse to get extra food, he pounces like a wild beast on the perpetrator, who gets no dinner that evening and perhaps not the next day, either.

We slurp down the liquid. Every now and then, when we get milk soup or when tangy, German Roquefort cheese comes with our bread, mayhem breaks out. Rapturous exclamations ensue as we await the pleasure with trembling bodies and bulging eyes.

Consumed as we are by hunger, we perceive unspeakably heady flavors in the swill, which in fact contains neither fat nor nourishment. Lying prostrate on the lice-infested wood shavings, eyes shut, we slurp and slurp with abandon. . . . The hot fluid permeates our tortured insides as our taste buds conjure up epicurean wonders. Never before and never since have I experienced the thrill of a morsel or gulp of food as I did in Block A.

Judovics and his clique are drowning in plenty. They are rolling in treasures: the rations left uneaten by each day's corpses all go to them, and on top of that, they enrich themselves unabashedly when dividing food. All this goes a long way. The block medic's fenced-off enclosure has boxes upon boxes of cheese and mountains of bread. The men of the "healthy" work division sometimes get cigarettes or tobacco at outside work sites. They are required to sacrifice this to the block medic. Behind locked doors Judovics eats away, a lit cigarette always hanging from between his lips. Here this is a breathtaking luxury. Judovics has done so well procuring tobacco that sometimes even the Ältesten and doctors turn to him for little collegial loans. Every day, the disinfection men iron his striped prisoner's uniform, which is adorned with the handwoven insignia: *Blocksanität* [Block medic]. They get extra soup for doing so.

Judovics doesn't give his subjects even a passing thought. Addressing him is dangerous. His power grows proportionally as new arrivals stream in. Deportees arrive in ever greater numbers from other camps. It seems that our transport only got things going. One after another I see old comrades from Eule and Fürstenstein. Arriving from Eule is a gaunt Gleiwitz. At first I can't tell who he is. The face of this tall, thin man is so bloated that it's unrecognizable. Fogel the tinsmith, too, looks so different—his body covered with sores, pus oozing from dirt-filled wounds.

Two others, originally from my region, also arrive: Bergman, a lawyer, and Herz, the retired postal official. But in what condition . . .

In Eule they were inseparable, and here, too, they manage to squeeze into the same bunk. Both are among the careful. How they protected themselves! How meticulously they portioned out their bread! They even washed daily, though it meant less time for rest. From the food they'd saved up, they were able to have lunch and dinner in their quest to preserve the routine of life back home. Neither is a smoker, and this was a big advantage. Back then I witnessed their exertions with sympathetic disbelief, and now, on seeing them again, I have a painful sense of satisfaction at having been right. Bergman is obviously on his last legs. He can no longer move his swollen hands. As for Herz, he has diarrhea. Bloated, dome-like lids now droop over his searching cold blue eyes, but he still holds out hope. Yet again, they thought they were heading to the gas chambers, and lo and behold, they wound up here.

"The devil isn't so bad, after all," says Herz, forcing a smile.

I reply honestly:

"No indeed. Just bleak."

"This is a sanatorium," he says with a sigh. "You don't even need to slave away."

"But you don't get anything to eat."

"We can lie in bed. They bring the soup right to you."

Why should I disappoint him? His optimism is as incurable as his diarrhea.

The pace of work has slowed in Fürstenstein, say those who've arrived from there. By now, Sänger und Lanninger is operating at half steam, and even the castle demolition is slowing down. New human labor is just trickling in, while more and more people are breaking down. The train returning the Fürstenstein camp commandant from a holiday was bombed at a railroad station. The inventor of "Appell in the Rain" was no more. Before even our own time. Another sergeant took over command, one much more indifferent and less inventive when it came to contriving tortures. Berkovits's and the clerk's stars shine more brightly than ever before. The new gray one has put them completely in charge of the camp—and of himself. All day long he is holed up in the office barrack, immersed in the Nazi Party newspaper, the *Völkischer Beobachter*. He is looking for encouraging news.

Encouraging news . . . Thirstily we drink in the sensational headlines. And yet we don't believe the biggest ones, even though those arriving from Fürstenstein all insist they're true. Could it be? Was there really an assassination attempt against Hitler? It happened recently, confirm the newcomers, saying that they saw with their own eyes the official report in the *Waldenburger Zeitung*. They add that not long after the news, from one day to the next, the Wehrmacht's green uniforms vanished. Even the Wehrmacht soldiers have been cloaked in gray. SS uniforms, complete with the death's-head emblem. We too have noticed this, for it's happened here just the same.

What does all this mean? The beginning of the end?

I want to get off the bunk, to leave the block in search of more detailed news. I want to find people I know. I descend into the squelchy stream of filth, looking for a spot to cross. Since they brought me here I haven't gone farther than fifteen steps, even though going out into the yard, which is surrounded by barbed wire, is not prohibited. I have yet to go there, however. Since I am naked and it's bitterly cold outside, I couldn't go much beyond the door even if my legs *could* carry me. But they can't. One time I tried going up the stairs toward Block B. I was looking for tobacco. I buckled on the first step.

Humiliated and helpless, I look up into those heights a few steps up as if at the Himalayas. It is a moment of realization. Perhaps it is then that what I'd never wanted to believe while lying in the bunk registered in my consciousness: I don't have much time left.

Even now, I get nowhere. The bunk has by now taken me prisoner: I am afraid of the ground; I recoil at the thought of the demonic audacity of taking a step. Clenching my teeth, I try again and again anyway, hoping to do so at least within the block.

I learn to walk. How strange...The first time around I learned to walk, I did so from my mother's arms. Now it is the will to live that teaches me.

The ice-cold air of the hall makes me shudder. Dizzy, I drape my blanket, sparkling silver from lice larvae, over my head. *One, two... Left, right...*

I'm scared. Wearing a blanket is strictly prohibited, too. If a doctor or other bigwig catches me breaking the law, I'd be playing with my life, which is fading as it is.

This exercise demands serious exertion. By the time I flop back down on my bunk, I feel as if I've gone miles.

I find a new neighbor in my bunk. He was moved here while I was away from my bunk. I am in my eighth bunk since living in Block A. This one is close to the door.

Having a new neighbor isn't a surprise. So far I've had to report eight corpses in the mornings, which has meant—among other things—that I've passed eight nights pressed up against a cooling cadaver. You can get used to anything. Close quarters of this sort have meant being there as every dying man soils himself in his final moments, and sitting up a corpse to get extra food.

A parchment-hued young man stretches out beside me. Motionless, he stares up high, at the flywheels left over from the hall's days when it was full of machinery. He is wearing underpants and a shirt, a jaw-dropping rarity. He is clutching a narrow strip of linen. At one time we'd gotten such shreds as towels back in Eule, but ours had been confiscated on arrival here. There's an enamel mug in his rag.

These mugs are among Dörnhau's most esteemed possessions.

No one knows how and from where they wind up in the camp, but owning one is a sign of indisputable prosperity. Their market value: two portions of bread. Aside from the bigwigs, only those among us most adept at saving up for trades are able to strut about with a mug.

I turn toward him and speak:

"Diarrhea?"

He only nods. On his face I glimpse the unmistakable sign. *Facies Hippocratica.* I see it on a great many faces every day. The stamp of death. A stiffening of the lineaments, a marble-like glaze on the skin. Drooping puffed-up eyelids, like someone disfigured by lionitis.

He struggles up.

"Will the bread be long in coming?"

"They're handing it out now in the first row."

"I'm very hungry," he sighs.

"I know, buddy. Patience. It won't take even a half hour."

"Half an hour . . . I can't bear it that long. I'm done for. . . ."

"Sure you can bear it. We can all bear it. Me too. Steel yourself. What camp did you come from?"

"Kaltwasser."

"What are you? A student?"

"No. A rabbi."

He must have finished his studies not long ago, that's for sure. A rabbi. So he led one of the small religious communities in the Carpathians. I've forgotten the name of the village he was hauled off from, but even today I can see the young rabbi's face. Now and always.

There's nothing rabbi-like about him anymore, nothing human. No longer does he think of God, whom he'd once committed to serving with dedication; nor of the grandiose folio books of the seminary; nor of the Arc of the Covenant with its spidery gold Hebrew letters; nor of his mother's face.... He is thinking of the slice of bread from which he awaits life.

Again, he tries getting up, but he falls back down.

"Will they ... be long ... getting here? ... Give it ... to me ... already ... you cursed beings!" he utters, gasping. "Bread ... I ... my insides ... are bursting...."

A ghastly lukewarm puddle spreads out slowly on the sack of wood shavings under him. He looks at me. I, at him.

"Just hold on," I say to encourage him. "All of us are hungry. Surely you can bear another couple of minutes."

He waves a hand dismissively.

"I can feel myself getting weaker ... always weaker."

He now speaks more coherently, but in a barely audible voice:

"Can't I get it ahead of my turn? Maybe you could have a word with them up there.... If only they saw what condition I'm in ..."

"Impossible," I say. "You just got here; you don't know Judovics. In the best-case scenario he'd give me a good kicking."

He mutters Hebrew words, and then whispers clearly, in Hungarian:

"Good-for-nothings ... my brothers ... good-for-nothings ..."

He says this, and he breathes no longer. The veiny hand clutching the mug goes limp, and the vessel clatters to the floor under the bunk. The rabbi's eyes are open. They remain locked on me just as they were a short while ago.

The eyes are triumphant in their frozen stare, as if asking, "Didn't I tell you so?"

It's an unwritten law in camp that the belongings of a dead

person—if there are any—are inherited by his closest neighbor. But not even that is a simple matter. One must engage in physical struggle with those nearby for the pitiful stuff. A scuffle invariably erupts around fresh corpses. Stunted arms get tangled up; fingers snatch toward eyes; feeble blows land every which way. A farcical, wretched battle of frogs and mice. Those who are hit hardly feel it.

Indeed, three or four hyenas are now frisking the corpse. They even look inside the mouth, with yearning glances looking for the glitter of gold teeth. Sometimes such hyenas boldly act on their own. If they get their hands on a suitable tool, they break off a tooth before the corpse is carried away. The venture is risky but enticing, what with the prospect of a juicy and immediate profit. The kitchen workers are always ready buyers. On the other hand, those caught red-handed are beaten to death on the spot, for in such cases the bigwigs, who feel as if they've been defrauded, are even less apt to show mercy than in the event of bread theft.

But there are no gold teeth in the rabbi's mouth. The Pole on an upper bunk to my left hasn't stirred for hours, but now he slithers over, opens the corpse's shirt, and scratches about on the dirty chest with greedy fingers. He's naïve, looking for a secret stash of bread. The mug and the strip of towel have disappeared.

Another dead bunkmate it is, then. Yesterday it was a sixteen-year-old kid from Budapest beside me who got the numbered tag on his toe, and the day before, some acquaintance from Bačka I didn't quite recognize. I think he was called Freund. The poor guy had dragged himself of his own accord up close to me; he'd wanted to see a familiar face if the end came. Because it's not just looking at each other that we see who will and who won't live to see the next day. It's not just that the disfigured, lionitis-like face that gives it away. Those moving on feel it, know it, with heart-wrenching certainty—as did both light blond–haired, sickly Freund and the wide-eyed young rabbi I didn't know, the servant of God who'd been hounded to Dörnhau.

Sanyi Róth is also headed toward this fate. This time, officially, for he, too, is now one of the inpatients here. He didn't ask me to give him back the cabbage, and he's not shocked by what he sees. Sanyi Róth doesn't get shocked; he just reconnoiters. He makes do even here. Despite being an inpatient, he lands a position. As a corpse stripper. A repulsive trade, but this burglar with nerves of steel doesn't care one bit about such fine details.

He wears his blanket like a hooded cloak. On it is the badge of distinction shared by all: a roundish silvery splotch. Lice larvae. Sanyi also has underwear.

Physically he is broken like the rest of us. His hard face is marred by swelling, which is spreading dreadfully. Moreover, he complains of excruciating pains around his kidneys. But his nerves—so he says—are impeccable.

"If only my body were in the shape my nerves are in," he is apt to say.

He forcefully shoves aside the hyenas and then proceeds to undress the corpse. The job is profitable—Sanyi Róth always knows what he's taking on—for a certain percent of corpses have underwear. Underwear is serious currency, and the corpse stripper gets it. The rabbi has not only underpants but also a shirt. On arriving here he no doubt somehow managed to save them from the hands of those people confiscating clothes.

Róth peels the rags off the stiffening body. He works with speed and skill: within moments, the corpse is naked.

"Now we'll wash it," he says, folding the stained underpants, "and then off to the market it goes! I'll collect eight to ten a day. Not much of a job, but what's to be done? I got it through Józsi Pepita."

"Who's that?"

"Józsi Pepita from People's Park, in Budapest. You haven't had the fortune to meet him yet? You're lucky. He's the group medic up in B. He gives the whole block the jitters. He's a good buddy of mine."

"Pepita . . . What kind of name is that?"

"A stage name. He's the one who talked up the bearded lady at the freak show in People's Park. 'The show's on all the time; step right in. . . . Just ten fillers! The show's on, fine family entertainment! . . .' And now, my friend, I'm telling you, Józsi Pepita is a bigwig, and how!"

He tries to put on a face of devil-purging good cheer, replete with slangy talk:

"A silky set of underwear like this is always worth two butts. As long as there are cigs in the camp at all. Seems that won't be for long. Not much is coming in. Trading is freezing up."

He looks at me. Something occurs to him.

"Of course you don't have underpants, either," he says. "Here," he adds, throwing the just-removed rags my way. "I've got two good ones for when we go home."

"Thanks, Sanyi, but I don't need it. I can't put it on like this, and I have nothing to wash it with."

"Don't be crazy! Do you think what you see on me was

delivered from the laundry? Ironed, wrapped in pink tissue paper?"

"Just give it to someone else."

He isn't offended. Perhaps he's glad his fit of generosity didn't cost him much.

"Whatever, I won't twist your arm. Tonight I'll be back here at the bunk. Maybe the guys who go out to work sites will bring some tobacco. Can you stand up?"

"With difficulty."

"Got anything to sell?"

"No."

"No problem. I'll tell you all about that stunt we pulled on Lenke Square in Budapest. You know, the one I talked about in Fürstenstein."

He stuffs the underwear-bounty under his arm. He too is unsteady on his feet. I know he hardly eats. He spends all he has on tobacco.

He doesn't come back, neither that evening nor the next day. Never again. Later on I hear that he had kidney failure and couldn't stand up. "Dr." Grau operated on him.

He's finished, I conclude, imagining the unwashed paws of that unhinged half-wit and the wooden bench serving as an operating table in the doctors' room.

I venture over to his bunk. He is no longer there. After the surgery he was placed up in Block B. I couldn't go after him there. I was farther away from mastering the acrobatics of walking up stairs than ever before.

My grim prognosis proves exact. Sanyi Róth suffered to the end amid inhuman torment the day after the "operation." Those from Block B say this big man's death throes were unusually drawn-out and difficult.

That night his hollering drowned out the whole chorus of the dying. His bone-piercing screams diluted his pain. In his final minutes, some sort of spasmodic will to live took hold of him. He insisted on having a doctor, a doctor who'd help him.

"A week's worth of my bread to anyone who brings a doctor!" he shouted above the concert of the departing.

Braun, Block B's dreaded chief medic, a former professional gendarme and one of Sanyi's high-ranking patrons, quietly observed:

"Well, even this isn't such a good business deal."

Only toward dawn did Sanyi quiet down once and for all. His successor, the new corpse stripper, pulled off his underwear, which was in relatively good condition—obviously he'd kept the best on himself.

17

THOSE IN A NEIGHBORHOOD OF FOUR OR FIVE BUNKS CAN
carry on contact with each other without anyone getting
up. In this small world something unfolds that, in rare moments
of sanity, with much goodwill, we can call companionship.

At the start of December, yet another move. I wind up at
the front of the hall, right by the door leading to the latrine.
Mr. Salgó is the group medic there. He is a sixtyish, heavyset
fellow, a merchant from the Košice region. Locals from there
who'd wound up in top camp positions themselves had gotten
him this profitable post. Just how he'd dodged the draft of death
at Auschwitz—how he'd evaded Auschwitz's Scylla and Charyb-
dis, those monsters of the deep from Greek mythology—will
forever be a mystery.

Unusually for someone of such rank, he shouts only rarely
and his blows are few and far between. However, he is even more
unabashed than his peers in depriving us of our fair share of
bread and bonus food. He might as well be beating us. Being
in Mr. Salgó's group is not exactly fortunate. Indeed, after New
Year's even the block medic thought his brazen thefts were getting to be too much. It got to the point where Mr. Salgó was
no longer sharing even a gram of anything containing fat. An

investigation ensued. Found hidden in his bunk were two kilograms of margarine, a whole lot of sugar, and other foodstuffs. Since only our most prominent bigwigs—Lagerältesen, the head doctor, the block medics, and the Blockältesen—had the right to hoard, the old thief was demoted and fired. As far as I know, liberation found him still alive. His previous fat-skimming post had allowed him to get into shape for this rare achievement.

In my new location I've got some acquaintances within earshot and eyeshot. Bergman and Herz have also finagled their way here; Gleiwitz is lying about and so is Pali Nébl, the onetime owner of four hundred acres of lush Bačka land, the village tycoon. Back home, on account of his extravagant behavior and stinginess of comical extremes, Nébl commanded little affection. Here, too, is Morvai, the painter from Košice. Supposedly he was crazy back home, too. Now he no doubt is. Unlike the others here, he is not bloated and he doesn't have diarrhea. But he does have a fever. His facial bones are bulging out like incandescent spears; the whole man is being broiled and boiled in his own heat. Written all over him is the final stage of ravaging TB. There is no thermometer, but it's apparent that his fever is constantly high. His every thought and inquiring word concerns eating. Aside from that, he sleeps. He is ever selling his soup and his bread days in advance. He will let anyone have his next day's ration in exchange for two potatoes or a little bit of carrots. Naturally, there are always takers for the favorable transaction, so Morvai's portions are always being snatched up by creditors.

Whenever he succeeds at making such a miserable business deal, he pulls his blanket over his head and chews long and lustfully in the darkness. He then immediately falls asleep. On rare occasions he sticks his head out from under the blanket, without a word. His trembling fingers draw visions in the air. But mostly he sleeps. He barely has human form.

Izrael was a wholesaler. Back home he commanded prestige and power; here he is a nobody among nobodies. For days on end he doesn't eat. For his rations he buys tobacco; indeed, he even acquired a cheap tin box to keep it in. He tumbles along the pinnacle of nicotine madness toward imminent, certain death by starvation.

I too—despite my every vow not to do so—often sacrifice half my bread or else opt for another half ration (a whole ration is more prized than two halves), committing unforgivable frivolities for the illusion of nicotine, but compared to Izrael and his friends, I am but a second-rate copycat.

Izrael's eyes are afire with deadly fever, and he hardly has a voice. He got here much later than I. We were together for a while in Fürstenstein in the tunnels of Sänger und Lanninger: for much of that time, he was the rail cart operator I worked with. Never did I behold a more tragic and simultaneously more grotesque sight than that of this bald man with a furrowed forehead on the bumper of one of those little carts careening downward. A few strands of his gray hair would be fluttering in the wind, and it seemed that at every moment he wanted to plummet right out of the swaying cart.

Now he bids a final farewell from his carts, from business, from tomorrow. Listlessly he watches the inferno all day long, and every night he tosses and turns. He says more in his sleep than when awake. Like so many others here, he speaks with loved ones left back home. With those back home—who didn't even stay back home. They too have been taken away by German trains with securely locked doors.

Screaming above me is Handelsmann, the collector. He is nearly as old as Mr. Salgó. He is maniacal about bread, for which he trades soup, bonus food, and potatoes. He buys it with objects inherited from the dead and with anything that comes his way. Not for his belly: he collects. He has a grimy sack for bread, which he coddles all day long, like a miser with his gold. He is ever counting the dried-out, rock-hard slices, caressing his treasure, taking pleasure in it. He is one degree crazier than we are, and yet there is a steely logic in his madness.

Handelsmann is amassing assets, as he did back home. Assets open every door, after all. The treasure is hope and security, a hiding place and an emergency exit. When one day he has enough bread, he'll buy freedom with it.

The whole block knows him; he has regular suppliers. Through some nephew of his who works in the kitchen he gets special soup every day and lots of kitchen scraps but trades in all of it for bread. And yet at night his stash is regularly stolen from under his head. At such times Handelsmann is seized by a fit of rage. Being near him is dangerous. He lets out shrill screams, tears at his gray hair, and, sobbing, seeks something to kill himself with. It takes hours for him to calm down somewhat. At the next distribution of food, though, he starts collecting bread from scratch.

A few dying Greeks and Poles complete the circle of this sad neighborhood. We know barely a thing about those farther away, on other streets. No one gets off his bunk too often: amid our own misery we chew away at the lead-footed hours that pass, from distribution to distribution. Our "community" is not enduring: newcomers are continually being squeezed into the places of those who have died. Also, people are constantly being moved, which likewise affects the makeup of the neighborhood. Bunks are in short supply; not even our bigwigs' attempts to relieve the situation with these new arrangements do any good.

New people come every day. A wretched flood of the totally exhausted, from all directions. Forced marches often lasting several days only further undermine the newcomers' already-fading vitality. Many are murdered en route by merciless cold or even more merciless starvation. Our new neighbors no longer arrive on trucks. Trucks were a luxury, back at the start.

Dörnhau has become a hub. It is here that the land of camps had poured its expended manpower. Pariahs drained of their strength and whom the Nazis, in the grips of the psychosis of anxiety that comes with sensing the end, did not dare or did not want to put to death on the spot, according to their time-tested method.

Despondency and puzzlement take hold of the gray ones all over the camps. Work on fortifications ground to a halt everywhere as the delivery of materials thinned out. The news from the front appeared as dark clouds; no longer could the beauticians at general headquarters successfully apply their cosmetics.

Members of the SS hardly show themselves within the barbed wire. With the hallmark discipline in their blood, they see to their duty in grim silence, but in their free time they retreat into their quarters, which they leave only when it comes time for food distribution.

I can see them through the window, heads hung, lurching along with their mess kits toward the kitchen barracks. Their steps are not cheerful.

The junior officers come rarely, too, and yet we still turn pale when one of our bigwig's shrill *"Achtung* [Attention]*!"*—rings out. You can never know what might happen at such a time, what the outcome of the inspection will be.

Especially when Hans comes.

Hans is blond and wears glasses. He is practically a kid. A one-star SS officer, the deputy to the camp commandant. We lie in our bunks at taut attention. For us, bags of bones that we are, this means lying stiff and motionless, faceup, legs stretched out, arms atop our blankets and likewise stretched out, hands straight, fingers stiff.

The gray one conducts an inspection. His style and behavior reveal not a trace of the effects of the disheartening news from the front. An automaton bearing the SS death's-head insignia, he is programmed for blind obedience. In a horribly reedy voice he scolds the medics, and hits a few faces. He is hunting mainly for food, tin cans, and wooden crates hidden in the bunks: though we're not allowed to keep anything with us in bed, in practice two cans live in peace—until they are stolen—beside the heads of most of us. One of them is *kosher*. We can get our soup in it when there are not enough earthenware bowls to go around. The other is *not kosher*, serving as a chamber pot. It is not at all unheard of for the two to be mixed up.

Hans—bent on ensuring hygiene above all else—throws out these indispensable items if we don't manage to hide them in time in our sacks that are filled with wood shavings. When he has the time and is in the mood, he is not averse to whipping the unlucky owner to a bloody pulp or even kicking him until he's half-dead.

This is Hans, who had not lost the war even in December 1944.

18

W E GET A HEAVY SNOWFALL FOR CHRISTMAS. JUST WHAT do *we* get? Not much—only the snowflakes coating the window frame.

Simultaneously with the whiteness a strange, oppressive atmosphere descends upon the factory of death. No doubt there is something in the air. The "healthy" labor division ceases going out to work: they are shiftlessly puttering about all day long. The Germans stop reinforcing their fortifications. The pace slackens; the treads of the wheels turning day by day lose their grip.

Encouraging news from the front is reaching even us. For a time, the SS soldiers depart from their usual, sullen silence; at least they are more communicative with the bigwigs. The approaching end renders them more helpless. They seek their better selves, and the motivation of self-justification rings out at every turn from the words they share in confidence.

"I, X.Y., personally can't do a thing about it. Orders, orders . . ."

Or perhaps:

"I said a long time ago that this can't go on. . . ."

In our bunks, though, we feel little effect of all this. Indeed, the frequent disruptions involving the kitchen staff, who have begun faltering in their duties, has rendered our vegetative existence even more uncertain. Even the usual sorrel and potato peels are now missing from our soup, and the bonus food is withdrawn from one day to the next. Over two whole days at the end of December, we don't get even our now-diminished bread ration, one-sixteenth of a loaf.

Death reaps an even bigger harvest. Bergman opens the new wave. He departs before New Year's, in a strangely easy exit meriting mention in a medical journal: He felt the same as always. He was talking. His chin dropped mid-sentence.

Herz outlived him by two nights. From our days back home I remembered this sought-after gray-haired gentleman who'd dressed with such provincial elegance as a living statue of methodical thinking and pedantry. The two of them, Herz and Bergman, understood each other, and their keeping one household at the camps—buying and consuming everything together—brought relief to both of them. They always worked in the same groups, together finagled their way to soups after complex calorie calculations and traded their bread for a spoonful of sugar or a drop of margarine. They were Castor and Pollux of Dörnhau, those twin half brothers of ancient Greek and Roman mythology. It would have been unimaginable for them not to undertake that final venture—death—together as well.

Bloated to twice his original size, unrecognizable, his body crippled—so departed Gleiwitz. Pali Nébl left us, too, his final minutes a frothing frenzy. He'd cast himself off his top bunk: a naked ghost. The agony that had built up in him raged with superhuman force. He began to run, pushing aside those in his way, shouting:

"Everyone, listen here! *Achtung! Achtung!* A slice of Napoleon vanilla custard puff pastry for every soup! Back home I'll give one for every soup! I'll put it in writing! I have two thousand slices buried there! People! Comrades! One whole slice of Napoleon cake for every soup! . . ."

He collapsed by the door. That was his end.

What could starvation have meant to this man? To be cast out from the overabundance of the village economy, from a land of gourmets, into the biblical seven lean years of this inferno that reeks of dung? I wasn't surprised that the final, farewell exertion of his decaying brain conjured up not abstract wisps of memories, but the splendor of chewing. To eat, even at the cost of gold hidden back home, only to eat! Eating is the apex of satisfaction!

In Dörnhau, doom has a hundred faces. The Grim Reaper has established an experimental laboratory in this hall of the decommissioned rug factory.

Here there is death by contagion. You die because you've seen your neighbor's death throes from start to finish. What's left of your own life force is infected. Indeed, every distinction between people in this respect has long faded. Everyone is now equally ripe for the end. The difference is hidden in the intangibles. Some still hang on out of sheer will, which has transformed into strength, while for others, even this has disappeared. Each day we are witness to the contagion of death.

Newcomers are settled in among us in place of Bergman, Herz, Gleiwitz, Nébl, and the others. Poles, Greeks. Also, two acquaintances of mine: Ernő Brüll, the lawyer and pianist from Slavonia; and Jancsi Fehér, who once volunteered alongside me in an editorial office and, later, during the years of occupation by

Horthy's forces, switched to far more profitable work: the black market.

Ernő Brüll is constantly crying. The onetime hedonist has softened and turned childlike. Tears are dribbling down his densely wrinkled face, coating his white spiky stubble with dew, flowing into his soup. As if compelled by a higher power to do so, he talks ever more of his mother.

"Believe me," he whimpers, "the only reason I'd like to get home is to see her. To kiss her blessed hand. And if they took her, if they took her away, too"—his face hardens—"I'd take revenge! Merciless revenge. I'd apply to be a supervisor at the labor camps they'll establish for Nazis."

The onetime favorite of small-town society now gasps out vengeance through his sobs. His eyelids are red from ceaseless crying.

Lively as quicksilver, Jancsi Fehér tries maneuvering. He seeks out contacts; he wants to be among the privileged. He forges plans, wanting to present economizing ideas to the Lager-älteste. But his plans, which worked well on the black market back home, are a failure here. The best he can manage is to wheedle his way in as a corpse registry clerk: within a certain district he's the one who registers dead bodies every morning. He gets a pencil stub, paper, and special soup. Nothing else. This doesn't satisfy his ambition; no, he focuses every iota of his will on a single goal: to make it. Not to make it home, but to make it. . . .

But he, too, fails. The body, that stubborn body of his, doesn't comply. By the third day he can't stand on his own two feet. He is unable to get up to tend to his rounds. Poor, ambitious Jancsi loses his pencil stub, rank, and special soup—everything. The strange yellowness of those with diarrhea comes over his child's face, and infirmity takes hold, his arms and legs as heavy as lead.

Just around then, through complex transactions, I get my hands on four big potatoes—an exceedingly rare delicacy amid the never-ending fast. For quite a while I struggle with selfishness, but finally I give in to Ernő Brüll's tearful pleading and offer a potato for the seriously ill Jancsi Fehér.

Jancsi is lying on the fourth bunk from us. Brüll gets off our bunk. He is back right away, the intended donation still in his hand. His tears have soaked the potato.

"He died just a moment ago," says Brüll, crying. "He looked at the potato. It was the last image he saw in this life."

It's as if our Poles and Greeks have no emotions. Even among themselves they hardly talk. This is not surprising, for they've been adrift in ghettos and camps for years, especially the Poles. Comradely ties among them develop with difficulty even between acquaintances and those from the same regions, and yet shrill curses are ever more frequent. Their bigwigs are a bit more merciless.

There are many fathers and sons among the Poles and Greeks. Sometimes a father attains a privileged rank, while the son remains a peon; or vice versa: the kid manages to become a lackey beside one of the bigwigs, maybe in the kitchen.

Hitler's slave strategy achieves the impossible. It penetrates the very primordial instincts of blood ties and manages to sever them: father and son fight over a morsel of food.

Examples abound before my very eyes.

An old Pole is lying on a bunk near me. His thirteen-year-old son wound up working for some Blockälteste. At first the kid paid daily visits to his father, bringing him leftover bread and also beets. At first. After a couple of days the hungry father sent messages, but in vain: the visits and donations dried up. When his old man died, the boy showed up once again, issuing threats, insisting on his inheritance.

A few of us are seething.

"You knew your father was dying, and you didn't even have the heart to come by? Have you no shame? Don't you even feel any love?"

"How was I supposed to come by when I had things to do?" comes the indifferent reply. "The Blockälteste would fire me if I keep running down here."

"But this was about your father. You knew that your father was dying!"

"And then? Everyone here is done for in the end, anyway."

Yes, this was the general consensus; every slave felt this. Here everyone is done for. . . .

We awake on December 31. One more night and the calendar will turn to 1945. Incredulously I pat my face, my hands, my legs. I am alive. Is it possible that I am alive? Those with more fervent willpower and stronger bodies have died and been removed from the bunks before my turn. I meanwhile am still able to move my limbs. I am talking and eating, and I am watching the spar-kling heaps of snow on the windowsill. My vision is clear, and I have notions about tomorrow. The bloating I arrived with from Fürstenstein has not subsided but—incredibly—has not spread. Up until now, diarrhea has spared me. True, for months now I've been careful not to drink too much water.

I feel in my every pore that events are unfolding. Something has stirred; something has to happen. It's not only contradic-tory, often chaotic bits of news that give me this impression, but also signs on the faces of our SS henchmen. My veins are pulsating with the sense of change in the air.

New Year's Eve is even bleaker than anticipated. We knew that an extra ration or another allowance was out of the question, but it hits us unexpectedly that the evening soup is withheld on Judovics's order, for "insubordination." We hadn't awaited the soup distribution in the requisite silence, and he happened to be in a bad mood. The men of Block A, hungry as wolves, take note of his inhumane "retaliatory" measure with hateful bitterness.

Meanwhile barrels of beer are being rolled from the food stall into the rooms of the bigwigs, whose gold-teeth racket has made this possible. Despair is on the rise. The skeleton-people are grumbling, threats and curses hissing all about. Gaunt fists are raised behind the back of Judovics, who, wearing a freshly ironed häftling outfit, parades between the rows of bunks with a cigarette between his teeth.

In the evening, during soup distribution, for once the lights are on. Márton—the chief medic of Block B, Judovics's colleague one floor up—is coming. According to people up there, he isn't as obstinate as the drunk-with-power, narrow-minded Judovics.

He is a polished attorney, eager for every opportunity to make a speech. He delights as copious, worn-out, convoluted, lawyerly sentences gush from his mouth. I once heard him deliver remarks beside the corpse of some friend of his, as those lying about nearby were paying limited attention.

He now clutches the table on which bread slated for distribution is kept.

"Friends," he says with exaggerated feeling, "I'd like to say a few words to you on the occasion of the new year that's upon us. Nineteen-forty-four was full of trials and tribulations for us all. They tore us away from our loved ones, forced us into slavery, and humiliated us in every way possible. Hundreds of thousands of us have been murdered and more are murdered every day. World history had not seen mass murder of similar proportions, and all of us know who is responsible for these horrors. All of us have heard news from the front, which can fill us with confidence. Of this—for understandable reasons—I can't speak here in more detail. Suffice it to say that the hour of freedom is not far; the year to come holds in its womb the day of our returning home, the moment we will see our loved ones once again. Friends, after these years of biblical suffering, may the Lord God grant us all a happy new year!"

The interpreters translate the short speech into both Yiddish and Polish. We listen to these slick words with tepid indifference. The barrels of beer, the dinner we never got—that's what's going through our minds. And yet the mention of freedom has a certain effect all the same, and the conjuring up of home works wonders. A few palms come together in weak applause.

But this self-indulgent speech casts me into a hell-bent rage. I stand up on my bunk and start to speak as well—in a loud voice, addressing my words straight at Márton.

"Block medic, sir! I don't know if you've been informed that on this day, New Year's Eve, this block was deprived of food on account of supposed insubordination. It doesn't matter whether we were insubordinate or not. I and all others still able to think in this hell are convinced that we didn't commit anything deserving of punishment. Six hundred hungry men waiting impatiently naturally means noise. That's not punishable. And if it is, then not in a way that, in our situation, is more inhumane, more deviously cruel, than anyone could possibly imagine. The camp leadership is committing a lesser crime when beating our fellow men to death than now, withholding food rations from those on the verge of starving to death. I don't know who is responsible for the fact that today six hundred of us here—people just the same as the camp officials—are now embarking into the new year even hungrier than usual, and maybe to their deaths overnight. In all our names I openly declare: this evening's forced starvation is a shameful, dastardly act. No one among us who remains alive will forget it."

The interpreters don't translate this, but those lying in the bunks tell their neighbors who speak other languages what this is about. My brief oration has an unanticipated result. The block echoes like some musical instrument that had been struck. I didn't want to rile up the crowd, but the truth did just that. Everyone is shouting; a smoldering protest bursts out. People are choking back sobs, stammering curses, and brandishing their arms right in front of Márton's nose. He is taken aback. People drag themselves off their bunks.

"It's shameful; it's a disgrace! To speak of liberation and deprive us of soup! Our own people are doing so, not the Germans! But you executioners were having dinner here, huh? . . . We saw those barrels of beer! . . . May you all drown!"

A Pole with a scarred face leaps in front of the stiff-as-stone Márton.

"Here I am; go ahead and beat me to death! . . . You can do it. You're all scoundrels, traitors, renegades! . . . Some of us will survive, and then you've had it!"

Frothing Hebrew curses are showering down. I'm frightened. There can be no doubt, I've stirred up a storm, and this cannot pass without consequences. The bigwigs' prestige is at stake, and they jealously safeguard that above all else.

Fortunately, Márton doesn't regard this breach of discipline as a calamity. He had no idea about the matter. Depriving us of dinner had been Judovics's idea, and it was all the more preposterous because no one even stood to benefit. The huge amount of unused soup would have had to be thrown out.

"Who was that talking just before?" asks Márton, beginning his inquiry.

I speak up.

"Your number?"

I tell him.

"What were you back home?"

I tell him that, too.

He turns away without a word and agitatedly confers at length with Judovics. He is clearly furious. After 10:00 PM the soup kettles are delivered. The triumph is complete, but I don't have much of a future with Judovics. The despotic stripling would not remain "in debt" to me for long, because the next day the higher-ups also got wind of what happened and Judovics gets a thorough "reprimand" from the chief doctor. In Dörnhau that means a few good hard slaps and carefully directed kicks.

Our block's little god nearly falls out of favor. Only nearly: I still have to be prepared for the worst. I conclude that it was rather stupidity, not bravery, to call upon myself the rage of the man who had a thousand comfortable, legal means of running me down.

All this doesn't come to pass, though, since commotion erupts—curiously enough, the next day, just as in Eule, after

Feldmann's assembly. Some of the sick, all those judged fit for marching, are to leave the camp. They are to head off soon. Destination unknown.

The order comes in the early afternoon. Our camp is once again a swarming bees' nest. Obviously the Germans are on the run. The camp's partial evacuation suggests that important events are unfolding on the nearby front.

In the afternoon I have a visitor. A well-nourished, smiling young man. He has Judovics lead him over to my bunk. His freshly washed and ironed häftling uniform bears an embroidered armband: Blockälteste II. I've never seen him before.

"Where is that newspaper reporter?"

I look up, perplexed. He addresses me amiably.

"I didn't know I'd find a colleague here in Dörnhau. I'm Bálint, a newspaper reporter from Bratislava."

I too say my name. This is the second time I have the opportunity to introduce myself to a bigwig by name.

"We'll try to take care of you as much as possible," he declares. He looks me over.

"You're in pretty bad shape."

I must look pathetic: his expression becomes one of concern.

"As much as possible, we'll make your situation bearable. As much as possible. Since you know . . . I've already spoken to Párdány, my cousin. You also write literature?"

"I've written this and that."

"I'll send paper and pencil. You can work. There are enough impressions."

"Work? Here?"

"You can write anywhere. Think of François Villon!"

"Yes," I replied, remembering the French poet of the Middle Ages who'd spent time writing from prison.

"You see."

He turns to Judovics.

"You'll transfer my colleague to the first row. On his own bunk. Is that understood? Extra soup and extra bread every day for now. You'll regularly report on his condition to the chief doctor."

Bálint comes down several times, and once even brings Párdány with him. In fact, my condition improves a tad. I get a disinfected shirt, underwear, and a deloused häftling uniform.

The interest Bálint and his clique show in my fate renders me immune from revenge at the hands of Judovics.

The recruitment of those who are leaving begins the next day. The Germans entrust this too completely to the häftling leaders. The examination is as superficial as it can get; it's more of a formality. Aside from a few primitive stethoscopes, the examining doctors don't even have instruments at their disposal.

They tell us openly:

"You can choose. Do you want to go, or stay? As you like it."

Grim alternatives. häftling marches, which most of us have experienced, mean almost certain death at this time of year, in winter, even for those in much better condition than the patients in the Dörnhau factory of murder. Staying here doesn't seem advisable, either. Rumor has it that the Germans, once they evacuate once and for all, will blow up the buildings with those remaining inside. Knowing Nazi methods, the news doesn't seem far-fetched.

Most opt to leave. Things can't get any worse anyway, they reason. Marching? Death? Let it come!

This becomes the prevailing mood. Dying people who never travel anywhere volunteer because the next night will be their last. Using indelible ink, the medics draw a big letter *W* on the thighs of those enlisted: *Weiter* [Farther]. Those remaining are marked with the letter *R*, meaning *Retour* [Back]. This stamp tattooed on the body stands in for a draft card.

I don't take much time deciding. I'll stay. I decided in the first minute and stand by my instinct. For now, most of the camp staff stay behind, too. The Lagerälteste, the head doctor, Bálint, Judovics, all of them. For now, then, there is probably no cause for concern. When I ask him, Bálint replies with great candor:

"Not even the SS know anything. They received an order that half the guards should head westward without delay along with the 'healthy' labor division and the sick who are able to walk. There is total chaos on the front. Soviet troops are approaching eastern Prussia. Russian battalions are fighting near Breslau, which is not even one hundred kilometers away."

"Aren't you guys going?" I ask Bálint.

"Not for now," he replies in confidence. "If we set foot outside of here, that's it for our ranks. Beyond the fence, we're commoners. Common pariahs. We'll wait and see what happens."

Those leaving the camp get real clothes from the Auschwitz stock. But not one has a coat. Nor is food distributed to them. Some forty of the doctors are among them. Quite a few officers leave, but Judovics remains.

Around two thousand men go out through the barbed wire–laced gate. A good number of the guards are with them, too. The gray ones are no longer bothering about order, not shouting as much, submachine guns no longer hanging from their shoulders. They are carrying revolvers; a few have rifles with bayonets.

The army of the departing twists along the sparkling blanket of snow on the road to Wüstegiersdorf. Many look back at the battered buildings here, which from a distance must look abandoned. They even look a bit sorry for those of us who have remained.

Few of them saw home again, however—far fewer than those who stayed.

* * *

Hundreds of others arrive the very same day. A flood of humanity pours into Dörnhau from Gross-Rosen, Kaltwasser, and Wüstegiersdorf. We are utterly perplexed. It seems this isn't an evacuation, after all.

Bálint shrugs his shoulders:

"The Russians are advancing toward Kattowitz. It seems to be complete chaos. The worst of it is that the new arrivals are bringing their own officers."

In fact, new henchmen appear, mostly Galicians, along with SS guards who induct them into their privileged roles here. There is a legion of Blockältesten, clerks, medics, doctors, kitchen workers, and other kapos. Lots of fleeing Lagerältesten arrive, too, so Muky is forced to share his throne with the newcomers.

The human shipments arriving by the hour ensure constant commotion. We're the ones who pay the price for that, too. We get our drastically reduced bread rations erratically, and frequent stoppages occur even in the soup distribution.

Uncertainty and impermanence. Every day, hundreds come and go. The enlistment continues. One or two divisions hit the road each day, so ultimately the number of those lying in the bunks is for the most part constant. We begin to understand.

All indications are that we've become a through station on the evacuation route.

The dead are no longer registered. If someone notices that his neighbor is no longer moving, he simply shoves the corpse off the bunk. Naked bodies pickle for days in the river of dung. Up until some gray one happens to come inside and have them taken away. Even this is worthless. Half an hour later fresh corpses are soaking in the pestilential puddle.

Uncleanliness takes on unimaginable proportions. The infected squalor envelops everything and everyone. Aside from the human waste that has not been cleared away, the penetrating stench of cadavers renders the air virulent. Discipline is increasingly lax; our kapo officers simply don't bother with us. They bother with themselves. Bálint still sometimes comes down, but even he can't help much. He's become my sole source of news. There's a big camp for women three kilometers away, and Bálint goes there weekly on official business. The women, especially their kapos, have more freedom of movement; they get more information about the outside world. And women members of the SS are more communicative.

One time they even send bread to Ernő Brüll, who has lots of personal acquaintances among them. The benefactor was someone he knew from Subotica. Things must have been going well for her, as she got an entire loaf through. Brüll cried tears of joy. He cried, like always. Aside from its value as nourishment, which can't be dismissed, to him that bread meant *woman, body.* Brüll then spoke of them, of women, those enchanting creatures who dole out pleasure.... He spoke of them for two days straight. His eyes sparkled as he chewed the bread, his faded gums conjuring up the fog of now-distant pleasures, the golden smoke of adventurers, the taste of women's lips. . . .

Women . . .

This is the first time they've occurred to me since I've been at the camps. Thanks to Ernő Brüll's good fortune. This is the first time I myself say the word, the first time I acknowledge the concept.

Thoughts about women mean nothing to the skeletons of Auschwitz. Desire fades away amid the shackles of animal instincts, the red-hot coals of hunger. The body can have only one desire: to eat. Nothing is important, just the rebellious stomach. Is there a worthier aim, a more enticing reward, than acquiring special soup? Is there ecstasy more vivid, more sensuous, than the smiling reddish-purple of a beet? A more intoxicating delight than that lurking in one's memory of fried potatoes?

There is no sexuality in the Land of Auschwitz. Overwhelmed by gastronomic fantasies, it leaches out of memories almost as if it had never existed to begin with. This unnatural absence, this demonic spell, derives only in part from physical weakness and the fact that we have not seen a woman—neither old nor young—for months. The reason is hidden more deeply. We've been living amid horribly disfigured, revoltingly deformed human bodies. In a chamber of horrors full of sores and boils oozing disgust. Our twisted imaginations debase our earthly vessels, our own bodies and those of others, into nauseating cadavers.

The underworld of sexual urges is generally unknown; indeed, its total absence would seem more probable. In Block A the sole, obvious exception is represented by Judovics, that well-fed

Judovics, who is free of worry over his next meal. His favorite is Michel, a puny sixteen-year-old kid, who has dark eyes as big as those born only in Andalusia and the alleyways of the eastern Polish ghettos. The girl-faced Michel has been through three ghettos. His parents perished in pogroms after the German invasion of Poland, and he soon realized that he could buy bread and other privileges for himself in the world of men living together in isolation.

The block medic coddles this stripling with an oafish smile in a nauseatingly open, ostentatious manner. In the light of day he showers smacking kisses on Michel's face and hands. He provides him with all the riches of his world, taking him into his fenced-off medic's enclosure. They clearly don't give a passing thought to the six hundred of us. Nor we, to them. To us skeleton-people, they mean no more than mere air.

After the liberation, Michel headed home with a considerable stock of gold, but he had an outbreak of latent typhus on the journey. He died in the home of a German peasant in Wüstegiersdorf.

Sexuality played a larger role in the lives of women's camps. This can be explained on the one hand by women's rich, deep sensuality and on the other hand by their ensuing opportunities for securing food. Their comparatively easier circumstances also played a part. The staff members at the male camp who went on business to the women's camps invariably found easy opportunities for romantic success. Bálint and his associates had regular girlfriends with whom they exchanged sentimental correspondence.

As with bigger morsels and better clothes, love also became the luxury of that narrow stratum, the privileged. The plebeians wasted away far from all this. All they wanted was to eat; yes, that is what they yearned for with lustful fire.

This was a sexual suspended animation akin to death, which was later followed, not infrequently, by the real thing.

For both Ernő Brüll and me, only now that we've been reminded do we remember such matters. Five minutes later, Brüll is no longer crying on account of the woman. He is tearing up because the soup he gets is even more empty than usual. In vain he fishes about in the thin liquid, but carrot slices are nowhere to be seen.

19

THE FIRST HALF OF JANUARY IS NEARLY OVER. YET AGAIN, our sole oasis is in planning our days ahead, for which the news we get provides an ever more realistic foundation. A couple of days earlier we heard that fierce street battles are underway in Budapest for the last blocks of buildings. A portion of eastern Prussia is already in the hands of Soviet forces, and in the meantime nonstop air raids have turned Berlin into a heap of ruins.

All this is lovely, but the question is, did it not come too late for us? Mistaken are those who believe that the slaves created by the Nazis still harbor a sense of community, that we cherished the promise of freedom for reasons in addition to our own, individual fates. Not in the least. We measured every development against the anticipated length of our own physical existence. We awaited peace; not so much that of the world, but our own. We began to fear the great peace mediator, death. Would the heart, my heart, not burst, would the body, my body, not become bloated, by the time the great turnaround rumbled its way here?

This is the selfishness of the primeval forest of filth and lice, the law of the jungle.

On January 14, I get diarrhea. Murderous spasms soon deprive me of my strength.

I toss and turn on the dung-colored wood chips. My lucid moments are less frequent. The fever plays a muddled, grisly horror show à la the famed Parisian Grand Guignol theater on a revolving stage of fog behind my eyelids. Staggering, I drag myself to the latrine. Ernő Brüll helps keep me on my feet.

Indifference. I do not wish for life, nor do I wish for death. Neither promises a thing. When I occasionally come to, I meet the ever-teary eyes of Ernő Brüll—my only sign of outside life. He speaks to me, but I don't listen. I don't sit up even at food distribution. By January 15 Judovics and his associates are sharing my bread ration.

It's a mathematical certainty that out of one hundred men at Dörnhau with diarrhea, ninety-five will die. Nothing more awaits me, either, but Ernő raises the alarm with Bálint, who, in a sudden flood of generosity, begins to shower me with the most opulent nutriments to be found in these circumstances. As first aid I get a one-liter tin can of horse fat. Every day, Ernő mashes up a nice big piece of simmering hot horse liver and forces it into me. With that, I quickly rally, greedily swallowing the fatty substance. The wondrous sensations soothe my belly, my insides. Around January 20 I am once again lying there open-eyed. I can't weigh more than thirty-five kilograms. My weightlessness sends me virtually fluttering into the air above my bunk. I am a shadow among the shadows.

I recall what I heard a doctor say lately. The key to it all is this: fat. Just about anyone at death's door can be yanked back to life with a quarter kilogram of butter or lard. But where to buy a quarter kilogram of that?

The fat and the barely boiled liver pour life into me.

"Back then Miklós got a great deal of liver," my schoolboy

memory quotes poet János Arany's epic poem trilogy *Toldi*, inspired by the legendary thirteenth-century Miklós Toldi, who'd served in a Hungarian king's army.

Indeed, I reflect, *liver poured strength even into Toldi. True, bull liver, but even that helps.*

Ernő Brüll and a few others are tending to me as best they can. Time is marching on; it's as if Dörnhau's seemingly dead Sleeping Beauty is stirring awake with the promising kiss of freedom and a renewed sense of solidarity.

It's not bad, lying there like this. To see nothing with open eyes, to feel my immaterial lightness, to lazily vanish behind the canopy of immortal indifference. And—oh, bliss!—to need nothing, not even cigarettes, to need nothing . . .

Healing. It seems I'm getting through even this. Outside, beyond the bars of the window, all is white. The barracks' grimy green is a bothersome stain in the sameness of the color of snow. Farther off, potato fields are blanketed with glistening flakes. Peasant wagons loaded with sacks, crates, furniture, and people have been clacking along the highway in an endless line for hours. Women and children wrapped in shawls, men cloaked in furs, animals led on ropes.

The last days of January. Ernő points at the line of wagons. Exultation in his voice:

"Look!"

I'm bewildered. *What is he happy about?*

"Refugees. They've been going on for days."

Silesia, adorned with so many camps, has become a veritable highway of refugees packed along with their possessions into wagons that are clacking along in a bid to outrun the rapidly advancing Soviet columns. A fire is raging at the arsonists' gate. The front has arrived here, behind the Reich's once supposedly inviolable borders.

It's hard to believe, but it's true. Those arriving from outside say the refugees even include Swabian Germans from Vojvodina's Bačka region. License plates on their wagons give it away, with place-names like Kljajićevo, Čonoplja, Crvenka, Odžaci, Gakovo, Stanišić, Riđica. . . . Germans from Bačka. They too have finally wound up here. They who, with flowers and richly laid tables, had welcomed the gray-uniformed, combat helmet–topped executioners, the murderers of woman and children bearing the SS's proprietary insignia. They who had pointed out the homes of Jews and Serbs—of so many decent, progressive-minded people appalled at what was going on—so that the apprehending squadrons wouldn't need to search for too long.

They have a lot to answer for, so they resettled here early on from the advancing Yugoslav partisans. But it seems they chose their new home poorly. They can't stay here, either, and now—with the possessions they scrounged and stole; with their women, children, and guilty consciences—they have been swept up in the quagmire of the migration unfolding here.

The avalanche has begun. Zhukov's divisions have penetrated the Brandenburg district and are within 150 kilometers of Berlin. The Soviet army is capturing smaller and larger German municipalities by the hundreds every day on all fronts.

Bluish-white phantom flames now flicker on the road each night: the carbide lamps of the line of wagons. Women are silently cowering; men are shivering and swearing; little kids are crying in their parents' arms. The line of wagons slowly burrows into the blackness. Airplanes zigzag overhead, on a curtain of stars. The drawn-out, plaintive wail of air-raid sirens can be heard from distant villages and towns.

There's quite a bit of traffic on the road even aside from that of the refugees. Furrowing through the dusty snow are columns of trucks; motorbikes; four-wheeled, open horse-drawn carriages of an antiquated sort seen only around here; sleighs; cars transporting furniture; divisions of SS troops and Todt's people. Hustle and bustle every which way; a psychosis of relocation in the air.

People are still streaming into our camp nonstop. A few are even somewhat able to work, having arrived from camps that have emptied out. They have been separated from most of their units, and now it's here, among us, that they are formed into new ones. They loll about, shiftlessly, all day long; work at sites outside the camp has long ceased.

The legendary Móric unexpectedly shows up. Until now we knew of him only through word of mouth, even doubting his existence.

Móric is the foremost kapo of all camps, the Lagerälteste of Lagerältesten, the führer of the death factories. The sole Jew in all of Germany able to move about freely in civilian clothes, without guard. He is a lank, pale Polish Jew. No one knows his family name. Originally he began as just the same sort of häftling as hundreds of thousands of his fellow men from conquered European countries. Just how he attained a position of such authority is anyone's guess.

He is the Jewish galley slave whose secretive connections reach all the way to the central German command at Auschwitz.

He is thus dreaded not only by Jewish slave drivers of all orders and ranks but also by German camp commandants.

He is a true inspector, invariably appearing without notice and then suddenly vanishing. He'd previously visited Dörnhau only once but had then thoroughly upset the trash heap of gold-teeth and food rackets and other such dealings.

He doesn't wear a Jewish symbol. He wears a surprisingly well-tailored gray blazer and a winter overcoat. There's a zippered briefcase under his arm. His lively, intelligent eyes shimmer with the hue of ancestral traumas. He doesn't seem healthy; word is that he has tuberculosis.

We now see him in Block A just once. He walks up and down the rows of bunks whose trembling occupants are lying at attention. With searching glances he takes in the sight. Beside him are the SS commanders; behind him, our Lagerälteste, the head doctor, and the clerks. He doesn't say a thing to anyone, nor does anyone dare to address him.

The silence is broken at one of the bunks. A dying man is wailing in prolonged anguish. He is bidding farewell to life in Yiddish, Moric's language, but the häftling king doesn't even glance his way.

When Móric leaves, Ernő speaks:

"You'll see, this visit means something. Anything. Some change."

Where Móric appears, there something must happen.

It does. The mysterious man, as during his prior visit, clamps down on the gold-tooth dealings. He demands an accounting. And after looking over the numbers, he quietly but very firmly removes the head doctor, Párdány, from his post. He names Lévi—a Polish medical orderly from one of the newly arrived transports—in his place. So too, he thoroughly curtails the autocracy of the all-powerful Muky. He doesn't demote him but places another Pole, Krausz, beside him with the same authority.

Likewise, Móric dilutes the army of clerks, kitchen workers, Blockältesten, and medics with newly arrived Polish Jews. He creates such upheaval in the already-disheveled ranks of the bigwigs that, by now, no one knows just who is in charge.

It's Bálint who tells us all this, the next day, after Móric has stormed off. Bálint himself emerges from the audit bruised. He got a co-Blockälteste.

Courtesy of Móric, we can now witness not only the raging, hand-to-hand tussles in the bunks, but—for a change—the repulsive fighting of the entrenched and new bigwigs who are now snarling at each other. Judovics's position alone has not been weakened. He too has been audited, but soon enough he gets through it. He goes on stealing the rations of the dying uninterrupted. His gold reserves are substantial.

Párdány, the toppled god, becomes our block's doctor. This may be an utter comedown for him, but it's good for me. Even deprived of his former throne, he's a bigwig. He still has his reserves, of which—when he is in a good mood—he sheds some upon us. Thanks to his contacts, he gets news from the outside world, and that, in these days of rapidly unfolding events, is more important than anything else.

Dr. Farkas is also here in Block A. He's been a blockmate for weeks, but we meet now for only the first time. My fellow serf with the Sänger und Lanninger firm, in Fürstenstein, he was in fact able to take it for a few weeks longer than me, even though when we first met he predicted he wouldn't be able to endure for long. Here his lot has improved; he got a position as a doctor.

He is an odd, tight-lipped fellow. A surgeon whose air of doctoral superiority—those measured mannerisms intended to calm patients—had been peeled away by months at Auschwitz. All that was left of Dr. Farkas was a tormented man like so many others affected by the circumstances here. He is alarmed to witness his supposed colleagues, the hustlers of his profession: dilettantes who've prostituted themselves, who've gone mad and are amputating with kitchen knives and stealing from corpses. When death runs amok from bunk to bunk, amid the nighttime commotion of Block A and the other blocks, they are deaf to the Hippocratic Oath.

He doesn't lose touch with the doctor in him, nor with the human being. There's not much he can do, but he sometimes caresses the length of a forehead bathed in sweat or repeatedly taps a finger over a fading pulse. With his reassuring smile and soothing words, he becomes the ferryman for those heading to the opposite bank. At risk to his life, he steals medicines from the gray ones' rudimentary pharmacies. With the sedative Evipan he lulls to sleep those writhing in pain, and he hands out charcoal lozenges to those with diarrhea. He doesn't become popular among us. Here no one can be popular; for that, we are altogether too indifferent by now. But the people listen to him, believe in him. When he doesn't come, he's missed.

Actually, I too only now get to know him. Amid the roar of the drills in Fürstenstein, his measured voice died away. The refreshing philosophy of his demeanor didn't have an effect. In essence, his philosophy: of all possibilities taken together, neither is life necessarily the best thing, nor is death necessarily the worst thing. Nor does he talk politics much; he's not keen on cooking up sham horoscopes about the prospects of our returning home.

"At the very least, a certain percent will get home," he tends to say. "Whether you or I are to be included in this percent is in fact immaterial." Looking down at his palms, which are furrowed and wounded all over, and at his fingers, which are full of boils and blisters, he adds, "And yet another thing is sure or, at least, almost so: it would be difficult for me to operate with these."

"Cheap cynicism," I argue. "I am I, and I'm not interested in any sort of utopian tomorrow if I can't be part of it. That much selfishness can still be selflessness. It's easy for you to talk in any case, since you didn't leave anyone back home."

Farkas is a bachelor.

"You're mistaken. Even unmarried men have mothers and fathers. I am certain that both my mom and my dad wound up in the gas chambers."

"Don't you even thirst for revenge? They knocked the operating knife out of your hands, but you can still get your hands on a pig stabber."

"Yes, but what good is that? A man can't punish. Who can guarantee that death is a punishment? Maybe life is."

"I can't look upon these things theoretically from a rooftop terrace of ideals," I counter. "Passions don't reason. And what remain of mine yearn for some sort of retribution. No, I no longer want to run the length of a street with a bloody knife. I don't want to punish a nefarious neighbor or fake friend or have him punished. He who turned away his stupid block of a head after the first anti-Jewish law. After the second one he sat himself down in your home and separated you from your father, your mother, your wife, your child; he certified you as being less than an animal. He stomped the human dignity you were born with—this remarkable, rightful inheritance, this wealth of yours—into the dung that covers everything here. He hounded you with an army of lice.

"Maybe it's all just curiosity," I continue, musingly. "What would *they* be like in this situation, after all? Would they like the taste of beets and potato skins? Would they be slurping down bunker soup so greedily? I'd like to see that smug, narrow-minded police constable here as he is picking lice off himself—that addlebrained, puffed-up cretin who added a lame pun to every name he read aloud from the list before departure in To-pola. Like I say, curiosity, that's all."

Farkas responds to my outburst with just an indulgent wave. He presses a little package into my hand.

"Multivitamins. Three times a day."

"After eating?"

"Instead," he says with a smile, adding, "Don't fool yourself into thinking that you're in such great shape. You may have gotten through the thick of it, but it's not as if there's much life left in you."

"And in you?"

"Not in me, either. In no one."

Someone is shrieking two bunks away. Dr. Farkas heads off. His wooden shoes are squelching in the muck. The official hours of death are beginning.

Judovics can't stand Farkas. Whenever Judovics can, he does Farkas harm: making sure he gets less at food distribution, and what's more, accusing him of "agitating" the new head doctor.

Farkas treats Judovics with deep disdain. Even our bigwigs respect Farkas's knowledge and his utter devotion. In short, he becomes a sort of liaison officer between the magnates and the pariahs. Miraculously, he sometimes even successfully intervenes on our behalf.

Judovics's perverse whims dictate how blankets, which mean life or death, are allocated. On account of the shameful approach Judovics has taken lately, Farkas has been kept busy. In some cases, one person gets two blankets; in others, two people, one. When Judovics is angry or gets upset at someone, he simply pulls off the collective blanket, calling it "disinfection." Since three-fourths of those people who are lying in the bunks are completely naked, this sort of thing isn't a laughing matter at all. The result is a resurgence of pneumonia. Farkas intervenes, and the Polish head doctor once and for all prohibits depriving blankets from anyone.

Judovics is furious, but he is compelled to obey. Moreover, the head doctor gives him a caning, too.

Thus the blanket torments end, and Judovics's hatred for the quiet doctor becomes even more bottomless. Compliments of Farkas, I too get my hands on another blanket. It is a godsend indeed, for it is freezing cold. Outside it's twenty below. The fading breaths of the hundreds in Block A provide no warmth. It's hardly any warmer in the hall than beyond the windows. Our daily death rate is more terrifying than ever. Newcomers arrive in place of the dead, only to become dead themselves by the next day.

We thought nothing more could happen, that the instrument that was this camp had no more notes to play. And yet it did.

I remember the day well: February 21. Farkas stepped to my bed. He was even more hunched over than usual.

"We just examined one of the Poles in Block B. High fever, delirious, shouting for water. In a careless moment he drank his own urine."

I stare at him. What's so unusual about this? Why is he telling me? He doesn't look at me. He says the word quietly.

"Spots."

The word is horrible to hear. An explanation is superfluous. We know what typhus is, especially in the cold crematorium.

"Sure?"

"Beyond a doubt. Five of us examined him. Every clinical symptom is recognizable. The tongue is typical."

Of course, the tongue, the tongue characteristic of those with typhus. An unerring symptom.

"It's a miracle," he goes on, "that there wasn't an outbreak a while ago. It seems the Germans no longer dare or want to commit honorable, straightforward murders. The date is too advanced. Death by cold—that's what they need now, to ensure themselves as little trouble as possible in their retreat. They want to carry fewer and fewer people with them."

Farkas's voice is choking with rage:

"Transports were directed here from infected camps. A simple, certain method. The incubation period is three weeks. They dragged the contagion into Dörnhau."

"And now?" I ask. "What will happen?"

"Nothing *will*. It's already happening. A typhus epidemic. With so many lice it should have happened long ago. The Germans didn't wait for that to happen. They gave it a push to be sure. Transports leaving from here will, according to plan, carry the contagion elsewhere. And here by tomorrow hundreds will fall ill. By the day after tomorrow, thousands."

Farkas's pessimistic prophecy is realized with uncanny precision. By afternoon, thirty cases are diagnosed just in Block A.

Panic everywhere. This time the bigwigs, too, have something at stake. There is no defense against lice, and from here on in the lice are carrying contagion. Our gray ones are in a frenzy. It's fine and well if the häftlinge die off, but as things now worryingly stand, it seems that they, too, have been left in a burning house along with those condemned to death.

They resort to simpleminded means of protection. At the order of the SS medic, a wooden fence is built with feverish speed around the infected block. A strict quarantine comes into effect. They lock us in a cage, but meanwhile they too know they are fooling themselves.

A new drama begins. Within a couple of days hundreds have come down with typhus. Doctors, kapos, Ältesten, gray ones. Indeed, the epidemic emerges among the civilian population of the surrounding villages.

Our doctors go up and down the rows of bunks three times a day. They measure pulses. If a pulse suggests a high fever, they carry the patient upstairs at once, to the hermetically sealed area of Block B. That's where they cram those who already have symptoms of the disease. The diagnosis is woefully crude. Even those whose fevers may have been conjured up by advanced TB, pneumonia, or other causes are thrown among those ridden with typhus. There are only three thermometers in the camp, and the doctors, who themselves are scared to death, hardly care about mistakes. Half of them have already wound up among those ridden with typhus. They "examine" from a distance of three steps, frightened to a frenzy of every louse as they are, though they know that all this is miserably in vain.

And yet Farkas seems to be in his element. He is veritably rejuvenated in the disaster. He straightens out his hunched back. He faces death defiantly, head-on. He doesn't dread infection; he nurses, he helps, he gives comfort to the extent possible. But it is less and less possible. The quarantine causes ever greater lapses in food allocations; the morsel of bread we now get isn't even enough for a tooth.

Our kitchen distributes an increasingly abominable brew in the guise of soup. Even the kitchen workers are in dread.

The gray ones aren't bothering about anything. Each afternoon and evening they lumber off with grinding steps through the crusty snow to the kitchen, steering well clear of the infected building. Otherwise they veritably entrench themselves in the administration pavilion. The convoluted threads of camp life come together in the clutches of Muky and his Polish associate. Governance and especially economic matters generally slip into the hands of Polish newcomers, who skim off what they can with even more shameless greed than their predecessors.

Diarrhea and edema are wreaking death, but by now typhus has statistically gained the upper hand. It ends lives more slowly and unpleasantly than the other two. A high fever for days and weeks on end, without major interruptions: we quickly learn that this is called spotted typhus. It's even possible to get better—in theory—if the heart can withstand the abnormally high body heat, if the weakening is balanced by suitable nourishment, and if the patient's surroundings are sound enough so that, especially in the first days, he can resist the frenzied delirium for water . . . if . . . And lots of other ifs.

Our two block doctors, Farkas and Párdány, both insist that not everyone necessarily dies of it. Everything depends on the heart. For now, they can't be certain since the process itself lasts the same as the incubation period: three weeks.

The tension is unlike any other: to be lying in a fenced-off death row and waiting, waiting for the moment when one of the lice swarming all around me will inject my blood with the fever. Brooding: *Is the disease already lurking in me?* Staring into the darkness, listening to the frantic chorus of those who've fallen ill.

The bunks fill up and empty out; the dead, and those with typhus, are carried away, and new ones are moved in. Once again, my days pass in a stupor; a numb half sleep cloaks the commotion of my nights.

Now, looking back, I can't even remember how I got myself through those days of March, though the disease hadn't even broken out on me. Again and again, I had to overcome one night of pestilence after another. With blood, with nerves, with physical strength. Those who were there and made it back home know that this was possible in but one way: by fleeing into unconsciousness.

The instinct to live throws us into a trance, often for hours at a time. Our sensations are sluggish; our consciousness is listless. We see and yet we can't see; we hear and yet we can't hear. This is more, and less, than being half-asleep.

Farkas doesn't mock me when I confess what's going on.

"That's precisely how it is. Escape into unconsciousness. Happy are those who find refuge there. I can't allow myself such a luxury. And yet being a doctor is in fact most beautiful of all in Dörnhau."

This is one tough man standing in front of me.

Not even the news from the front interests him particularly, but he spreads it all about tirelessly all the same. Today good news is medicine. It is a fever-reducing shot, a nourishing tonic.

Párdány, the ex–head doctor who lost his throne, is also surprisingly brave. He doesn't forget about me, either; sometimes he even gives me a few multivitamins, ones he set aside from his onetime days of splendor.

Bálint doesn't dare come down anymore. Our bigwigs are devoting all their time and energy to a single goal: to keep their beds, clothes, and bodies lice-free if possible. Naturally, that too is a delusion. The proportion of those who've fallen ill is hardly less among the higher-ups than it is for those at the bottom.

20

FATEFUL EVENTS ARE PILING UP OUTSIDE THE BARBED WIRE. Cologne fell at the beginning of March. The Allies have crossed the Rhine. The fight is raging for Berlin. Ten-ton bombs are showering by the thousands on German cities in ruins. In the second half of March, Frankfurt, Mannheim, and Danzig capitulate. After storming through Hungary, the Soviet forces are advancing into Austria and are at the gates of Vienna.

By now this is undoubtedly the end. Not only ours, but also our executioners'. I watch the gray ones as they feign indifference. They shuffle about with their mess tins; they even still hold drills in the yard. They're fussing about, busying themselves. What are they hoping for? From what miracle do they expect a favorable turn of events?

With the first day of spring, a new clamor bursts into the cacophony of the camp. Cannon fire!

It's hard to even believe. We imagine those dull booms as thunder, as explosions, as God knows what. Cannon fire seems impossible, after all. So soon? True, we'd seen the refugees and heard that battles were raging around Breslau, but Breslau is far away.

Ernő Brüll came down with a fever two days ago, and has been lying about mostly delirious, but now he too is all ears. He raises his head; in his eyes, the pure sparkle of consciousness.

"It can't be more than ten kilometers away," someone finally says.

It's hard waiting for Farkas, Párdány, and anyone else who might know something. We thirst for news, yearn for certainty. The proximity of the turnaround shakes the damp, leaky walls. The magnetic spell of hope shines in the first sunbeams of early spring.

Certainty comes. The Soviet forces are just outside Schweidnitz. That small Silesian industrial town is seven kilometers from us.

Our SS soldiers still seem indifferent. They are shuffling about the yard, methodically spooning out their wretched soup and smoking nasty makhorka tobacco from short wooden pipes. They don't pay us much attention, though they methodically lock the only exit every evening. Their armed guards keep watch in the night. At 3:00 AM the kitchen staff heading to work need to call out the day's password from inside. That's what it takes for the heavy oak gate to open up.

Our bigwigs are even more anxious. Our bottomless hatred for them is burning in our bones, and they can feel its heat on their skin. With alarm they turn away their heads as they read ominous threats in the eyes flashing their way.

Judovics is buying up belts and is having tailors make him a knapsack. A shoemaker from among the *Schonung*, prisoners deemed unfit for regular work, makes a sudden career for himself. From one day to the next he becomes a sugar and tobacco millionaire. He hires a lackey and gets his own bunk and a complete civilian suit. Though he smiles enigmatically, lots of people know the secret of his unexpected success: he puts melted-down gold into heels of shoes. In Dörnhau, capital is restless.

The Russians are meanwhile standing by Schweidnitz.

Alas, the emphasis soon falls on that word: *standing!* Two days later the cannons fall silent. We don't understand. Nor do our camp officials. Word has it that the liberators have stopped and have dug themselves in at Schweidnitz. So we must wait.

Others claim that Dörnhau isn't in the direction of the Soviet advance at all. They've gone around us.

Both versions are equally dispiriting. We receive the new blow with resignation. The bluebird of hope that's been winking at our bunks has again flown far away. The electricity of the instinct for life is gradually fading from Block A.

Disenchanted, we turn our attention back to picking lice off ourselves. We feel that the final chance has vanished into nothing. Once more the dying have no will to live; no longer do they grasp spasmodically at the straws of consciousness.

Starvation, edema, typhus . . .

Embittered, we shudder awake. . . . Here again is apathy, that numbing half sleep that sees us withdrawing into ourselves.

The camp staff postpones its packing. Transports neither arrive nor depart any longer. Newcomers don't occupy the places of our dead. The overcrowding diminishes and the bunks empty out at a frightening pace.

Nor is food served regularly anymore. The kitchen operates only at times, and even then just bunker soup is prepared. We get bread every other day. Provisions are dwindling, and there isn't even a hint of being resupplied. To make up for this we get two tablespoons of sugar a day: it seems the supply is larger. For those with diarrhea, sugar is poison, but they devour it greedily. The result: a rise in deaths among them.

There are hardly three hundred of us in Block A. The nights drag off forty or fifty every twenty-four hours. Another ten or twenty wind up in the typhus block.

Ernő Brüll is taken away, too. His fever has shot up to 41 degrees [105.8 degrees F]. The tears are now veritably searing as they ooze from poor Ernő's misty eyes.

Everyone around me has already been taken away. I feel it precisely when my turn comes: overcome with numb exhaustion on April 20, I accept it as inevitable. To a certain degree everyone always has a fever in the death factory, but this fire is something else. Typhus!

My consciousness quickly fades. All around me are spectral, terra-cotta figurines; Block A is a distorting mirror. Up above, near the ceiling, I see not what is in fact there, a dismantled flywheel from the hall's days as a factory, its drive belt removed but a spinning wheel revolving impossibly fast. Ghostly bodies seem to billow in a frothy cloud: these are the skeleton-people. The fever is a chisel pressed tight against my temple.

Farkas's ashen, elongated face emerges up out of the fog. He is tracking down those with typhus, seeing to his usual daily counting of pulses. As he leans over me, I can feel his fingers, cold to the touch, on my wrist. His voice comes from afar:

"Stick out your tongue!"

He calls over Párdány. They round up one of the camp's three thermometers.

"It's 40.2 [104.4 degrees F]," says Párdány, and adds, more quietly, "It seems every one of us is done for, after all."

Farkas is silent, but he doesn't leave the side of the stretcher on which I'm taken upstairs.

* * *

People, objects, all look as if they've been embossed. Typhus is like the rose-colored glasses of childhood. My consciousness returns; nay, it's sharper than it was down in Block A. Above forty degrees my temple is no longer an anvil for that hellish hammer. The first week of the illness brings a slackened, pleasant repose. Oddly enough, I am now not even tormented by thirst, which until now has beset me regularly. I feel light and alert. I'm able to observe the raging madhouse of fever like someone who has just peeked in here out of curiosity. I watch those possessed by can-can-like seizures. I listen to people shrieking, bleating, or whining, and those who are so humbly, timidly, begging for water. I observe the self-mutilators and the most ghastly of all: the anteater.

The anteater is lying two bunks away. A puny Greek, he looks like an old woman. He is not thrashing about, and neither can his voice be heard. But he is constantly turning onto his belly against the wood chips. He sticks out his cracked, white tongue and licks up the squirming lice underneath. The crunching is nerve-racking.

The days come and go, and I am awestruck to realize that, although I am dying, for me it isn't even so hard. There are more painful ways to go. For fifteen days now I've hardly eaten. Farkas presses a finger to my artery.

"Take it easy," he reassures me. "Your heart is withstanding it. That's the main thing. You'll recover."

"Is that important?" I ask, without expecting a reply.

But the doctor responds:

"By now—yes!"

I want to sit up. Farkas's lips form a half smile. No doubt, there's news.

"Do you know something?"

"Hitler's dead."

Brüll, who came down with typhus a week earlier than I did and whose fever is already on the wane, springs up like a jack-in-the-box. His tears spout out, as if by the press of a button. Now tears of joy...

"Did he die? Was he killed? What happened?..."

I'm suspicious. Maybe Farkas is putting one over on us. Merciful fibbing to a dying man.

"What happened? Probably just that—that the war is over. According to British radio, he committed suicide. That's the most likely. Berlin could fall any hour. Potsdam has capitulated. The Italian partisans captured Mussolini and hanged him in public. Well? What else do you need to know?"

We are now fully alert.

"How do you know?" we ask, besieging him with questions.

"The SS themselves are saying it. They've softened up lately. They're at a loss and in a frenzy."

"But they're still here?"

"Yes."

"And the Russians? Still at Schweidnitz?"

"Yes. But other columns are advancing as well."

"If they were close," I observe despondently, "we'd be hearing cannon fire."

The news is electrifying nonetheless. *To recover... To stay alive. To stay alive, now...*

Bálint doesn't dare to come up, but he wishes his best for

my recovery and perseverance. He sends a little sugar and margarine.

My fingers are as thin as matchsticks, and my knuckles are transparent. I wolf down sugar, margarine, bread that's accumulated, everything. . . . I have no appetite, but now it would be really a shame if . . .

Surprisingly, the death rate among those with typhus begins to fall. It's relatively fortunate that the outbreak is not the worst type possible. On average, one of every three patients recovers. Among those who got here earlier, some are even fever-free by now. According to Farkas, it's thanks to spring. The warmth of May doesn't favor the spread of epidemic.

Those recovered are let out of the typhus ward. They can return to their former blocks, which—by the way—they are not thrilled about. After seventeen days with an average of around 40 degrees [104 degrees F], my fever stabilizes at around 37 [98.6 degrees F]. Even Ernő gets better.

On May 1, the anniversary of our arrival at Auschwitz, both of us stagger back to Block A. During that short journey I am once again horrified to realize that walking is such a complicated operation. Farkas secures space for me near his own bunk. Not that I'm fever-free, but supposedly I've gotten through this. The space upstairs is needed for new patients.

Nowadays there are around two hundred of us in A. There hasn't been bread for days. Instead, we get two bowls of soup a day, as well as sugar. Here nothing at all suggests imminent liberation. The mill is grinding away, the camp machinery is still going round and round, like three months earlier. Even the disquiet of recent weeks has subsided. In fact, one of the healthy divisions has been sent outside again to work.

Filth and hunger continue unabated. To top it all off, abdominal typhus—typhoid fever—crops up. A merciful disease, it doesn't beat around the bush: it causes delirium within minutes, and death within hours. Párdány and Bálint catch it. Only Farkas resists, as if protected by a higher power.

May is oozing through the bars of the window. Those with sufficient strength to walk drag themselves outside. The yard fills up with people basking in the sun. It's tough for the rest of us, the bedridden, to be confined to the bunks, for the breeze carries the scent of spring, and milk-colored clouds are parading around the fresh-blue-polished sky.

There's an expectant silence in the cold crematorium. In the depopulating halls of the sick there are people, some of them mute; there are lice; and there is suffering. The bars around our bunks are dismantled. I quickly realize that it's unnecessary.

The bosses hurry in silence toward the latrine to tend to their business. Then they vanish yet again, not even glancing at us. As for the gray ones, all we can see of them are the silhouettes of the helmeted guards at the gate, and all we can hear are the steps of the submachine gun–toting sentry resonating against the watchtower's wood floor. Sullenly they huddle in their headquarters, even taking their provisions there.

There hasn't been tobacco for a long time. Strangely enough, I don't miss it. We don't even think of food with such voracious longing as before. The stimuli of starvation dissolve in the restlessness of anticipation. We feel that we are consuming ourselves, our bodies' remaining fuel. Our final reserves are keeping our hearts warm.

I can't sit up, but my vision is sharp. My senses are keeping me vigilant; my mind is working nimbly.

Farkas is now my neighbor. Together we are listening to the chilling cacophony of the nights, spying into the dark, awaiting signals from outside, awaiting sounds: the blasts of cannon fire and grenades, anything that points to the future.

No longer do we have news: we are completely cut off from the outside world. On May 3, the gray ones don't even let the food-delivery häftlinge into the administration building. They carry the cauldrons themselves.

Judovics is nowhere to be seen. He's moved up into one of the officers' rooms. As for Miklós Nagy, the sadistic young chief medic, he has typhus. The bigwigs are moving out of every block. They huddle upstairs, consulting nonstop. Feverish preparations are again underway.

Not even on May 5 are we asleep before daybreak. As has been the case for days now, we've been spending the night in hushed conversation. The watchtower's beam of light is blazing upon us from the window opposite. It's 3:00 AM, when the kitchen staff head to work. According to the rules, a call goes out from inside the camp to the sentry, who then opens up the gate.

We can hear the drawn-out call even now:

"Herr Posten, aufmachen! Drei Uhr! Kücjemarbeiter hier! [Open up, sir! It's three o'clock! The kitchen workers are here!]*"*

Some sort of password is called out, too.

The sentry always opens the gate at the first call, but this time he is inexplicably late. The kitchen workers impatiently pound away at the gate. Long minutes pass without reply. Without thinking, one of them grasps the handle and pushes it down.

The gate opens wide. The guards didn't even lock it.

During this night, for the first time after so many months, we had been free again—without knowing it. . . .

People rush outside. There is no one in front of the gate. The watchtower's signal light is on, but the guard is nowhere to be seen. There's no one even in the administration building, the local headquarters of the SS. The rooms are in disarray, with evidence of packing in a rush. The camp is empty.

Tearful shouting erupts from throats all around, spreading like wildfire in this house of death:

"They've fled!...The gray ones have fled!"

"We're free!...We're free!"

The blocks come alive. An unleashed deluge pours over one and all, a flood of inarticulate voices. A spiritual of sobbing surges forth from the May twilight. This dawn of liberation flares up in the cold crematorium.

The guards have fled!

Those who can are flocking to get outside. Months of established order melt away into nothing in the space of a minute. The now-absent discipline of the whip and revolver kindles anger and ignites fury among the häftlinge. No longer is the kapo a kapo; no longer is the dung-bucket carrier the dung-bucket carrier.

Hundreds storm the storerooms. They break into the barracks and devour or scatter anything they find. Others stage an assault against the arms and clothing depots. Screaming crowds press against the doors. Submachine guns, rifles, uniforms, work boots, revolvers, gas masks, rubber truncheons, cartridges, and hand grenades fly into a mountainous heap.

Praying and shooting, cursing and hugging, crying and laughing...Inarticulate sounds pour out of everyone and everything. A raving madhouse!

A bonfire is blazing in the middle of the yard. The papers of the SS office are flaming skyward. Everyone is armed to the teeth. Ernő equips himself with a submachine gun; hand grenades dangle from his belt. The spectacle brings a smile to my face: a well-armed, whimpering Tartarin, that iconic character out of nineteenth-century French literature. His tears now fall onto the stock of the submachine gun.

Twenty or thirty people hop on abandoned bicycles. They head to Wüstegiersdorf to look about. No one bothers with us, but the ecstasy takes hold of the bedridden, too. We would get up, but it doesn't work. When I try doing so, after a few steps my legs buckle again and again. I can hardly trudge back.

It's 8:00 AM by the time the chaos somehow lets up. We then awake to an intoxicating surprise. Our most hated slave drivers, those upon whom the collective thirst for vengeance bore down upon most—the truncheon-thrashing murderers, the gold traffickers, those who'd stomp on bellies with bull-pizzle whips in their hands—had slipped away, without exception and without a trace, in the nighttime upheaval. With their bounties to boot: exactly as they'd planned so meticulously well in advance. Indeed, they'd stocked themselves up with arms, provisions, and even German marks—which wasn't hard: wads of banknotes from the Nazi treasurer's office are lying in heaps in the yard. Judovics vanished with his lover, as have Muky, the Lagerälteste; Miklós Nagy, who slipped away from the typhus ward; and practically all of the Polish kapos.

Aside from their bounties and guilty consciences, they also took latent typhus with them. The disease struck them on the road; they spent months astray in hospitals and in peasant homes. Many perished.

The less compromised bigwigs tear off their embroidered armbands and try mingling in the crowd.

The newly liberated search in vain for tobacco and cigarettes, but they do find a few cases of virulently strong German cigars. I get one, too, but after a few puffs I get dizzy and fling it away. The gray ones did, however, have plentiful reserves of wine, liquor, and plum brandy. In no time hundreds of people are drunk. The alcohol quickly gets the better of the weak. Whooping cries thus find their way into the sounds of joy.

Someone staggers by the bunks and presses a burning cigar into the corner of the mouth of a fresh corpse. The fellow laughs heartily and stuffs his mouth with preserves of some sort.

Not that I'm squeamish, but I must turn away all the same. If I had a weapon, I'd shoot the vile stripling without a second thought. Nausea stirs in me, and I shiver.

It takes me quite a while to calm down. I search for the excuse—not for that drunken beast, but for myself, for all of us. Perhaps it is not surprising that at such moments we belch up the most hideous instincts, whose seedlings have been watered by paranoid barbarism so attentively over the course of the past six years.

So too, I seek to understand why, in that initial tumult of rapture, food and care do not find their way to the lame. The bedridden are now even more abandoned and the dying are dropping dead even more pitifully than yesterday. And yet the storeroom pillagers are up to their knees in sugar, potatoes, and canned goods.

Daybreak is fast approaching on this first day of freedom. We await the liberators, but they are not coming. Neither in the morning, nor in the afternoon, nor in the evening. Those making incursions into Wüstegiersdorf by bicycle and by foot flit back three times, packed to the gills. They even bring three passenger cars. They found them abandoned in the hamlet, and so they commandeered the small Opels, which are in good condition.

Wüstegiersdorf is uninhabited. Except for a few old people and those with typhus, the residents have fled. Only the panicking mayor, at a loss for what to do, has remained to receive the entering troops. But they have not yet turned up even there. Apartments, stores, and workshops are wide open. The local Nazi Party headquarters stands there, bereft of its decorations; gone are the swastika flags and posters.

Farkas has been in town, too. He reports:

"Those few people who've stayed behind have no idea when the Russians might arrive. I've otherwise been able to confirm that my old notion is correct: The Nazis are not only murderers. They are also cowards. Their bootlicking, which knows no bounds, is revolting. Right before our eyes they make a big show of ripping up and spitting on Hitler pictures. They have the gall to claim and even to swear that they hadn't a clue what thousands of people were undergoing in their immediate proximity. They believed that this was a run-of-the-mill POW camp; so they insist. Of course, they had no idea that millions had been deported. All this is naturally a despicable lie, for barely three kilometers away there's a women's camp, too. They must have known about that. . . ."

Those in Dörnhau cannot resist the opportunity. For years they had no personal possessions, so now the desire to own catches them in its grip. They go about collecting impractical, nonessential stuff indiscriminately, unthinkingly. They're hunched over from the weight of backpacks, suitcases, sacks, and haversacks. They loot cumbersome calculators, typewriters, medical instruments; they are dragging heavy rolls of cloth behind them. Most cast off the bulk of their bounty on the way back. It's heavy. Heaps of scattered, abandoned loot collect along the road. Consequently they bring that much less food. The German pantries are not well stocked.

Within the barbed wire fence: anarchy. The kitchen workers—understandably, from their point of view—refuse to work, though except for bread, the breached storerooms have provisions enough for several days. Those healthy and ambulatory patients who'd been tasked with cleaning, carrying off the dead, collecting dung in buckets, and distributing food have mostly left. Those among them who stayed behind are swaggering about with hand grenades and submachine guns. Only their consciences might compel them to continue their work.

Farkas and a few other doctors recognize the dangers of this anarchy. There are people here with typhus, the lame, the dying, and those now starving more than ever, who yet might be saved.

The doctors convene a few men and try persuading them to form some sort of temporary organization to manage the cooking and see to other daily tasks until the liberating troops arrive. Cleaning would be especially important. The yellow stream between the bunks is knee-high by now. The precautionary measures against typhus, which were rudimentary to begin with, have ceased. Taking action now is in everyone's interest.

Such arguments are lost in a vacuum. It's all useless; everything goes on as before.

The next day, our comrades start pouring in from Kaltwasser and the region's other camps. They were liberated at the same time as we were. The SS troops, probably according to a prearranged plan, withdrew from all the camps around here. Those traveling through here from all directions are in relatively good shape, and on the first day they resolved to embark on foot on the journey into the unknown, toward home. Soviet forces have so far appeared nowhere; typhus has appeared everywhere.

They talk enthusiastically about yesterday's big events, about their series of savage reckoning with the bigwigs. The camp officials didn't escape so easily everywhere as they did in Dörnhau. At Kaltwasser the hated Lagerälteste was formally sentenced to death and hanged in the middle of the yard. As he stood in the gallows, the condemned man asked for time to smoke a cigarette. His request was not fulfilled.

Many of the bloodsuckers who'd slipped out of camps were pursued and dispatched in shootouts, since the regular escapees also had weapons.

Nearly everyone from the camps that weren't used as hospitals went on the road. Where? The answer to that question was clear: home!

How? That much, no one knew. The galley slaves fleeing the camps weren't even familiar with the region they were in, nor did they know if there were still German units nearby.

Latent typhus cut down a tenth of these people heading home. For them, their venture generally ceased in some hospital along the way for months or, perhaps, forever. Not that any of this occurred to them when setting off, not that they knew it or cared...

The next afternoon, Farkas set off, too, together with Ernő Brüll. Ernő was always in much better condition than me; before getting typhus he hadn't even been bedridden.

"There's no other choice," the doctor concludes quite reasonably. "The first Russian medic or doctor to set foot in here will obviously place the camp under quarantine. In the best-

case scenario, that will mean a forced stay of weeks in this accursed, thoroughly infected rathole. Anyone the lice have not
yet injected with the fever will also get it sooner or later. Even
aside from this, the start of some official, organized repatriation
could drag on for months, if not a year. Taking advantage of
the initial chaos is necessary, since doing so later will be harder."

I must admit that he is right.

"Don't be angry," he continues. "I know this has the putrid
odor of leaving you in the lurch. I've racked my brains over how
I could take you with me."

"Naturally, there's no way."

"Alas. You'd die along the way. It's a wretched matter, but
what am I to do? . . ." He falters. "You know what it means to go
home . . . to be able to go home. . . . God be with you!"

The farewell is short. Ernő Brüll is sobbing. We hug and kiss
each other. With little conviction that it will do any good, we
exchange addresses. Addresses, fates, lives . . . Who knows where
they'll drift off to?

They leave two days' worth of food on my bed. It's welcome
indeed, for it's still uncertain when the liberators will arrive.
Will they come at all, or have we been left out once and for all
from the line of their advance? Even the immediate future of the
powerless is unpredictable.

21

THE WOMEN'S CAMP HAS BEEN LIBERATED. MANY DEPARTING women stop by in Dörnhau en route. They're in better shape than we are. All of them have already gotten their hands on normal clothes.

It's a hard night in Block A. Only the lame and the dying are left in the hall. The rest—if they haven't yet left—have moved into the rooms the SS left behind or else have occupied some abandoned home in town.

The solitude is oppressive and inconsolable. I fear for this life that is ready to fade. To leave now would be outrageously meaningless. . . . The helplessness is exasperating. I'd like to move, to leave. Clenching my teeth, I try again to walk. I think with envy of Farkas and Brüll, and yet I miss them. I miss the other faces, too. I miss everyone I ever spoke to. No longer do I know anyone here; new people I've never seen before are gesticulating all around me.

As if by the press of a button, within twenty-four hours a new aristocracy appears. The ephemeral monarchs of this interlude. Those who managed to build up the biggest, most valuable bounty. The knights of better clothing and more canned goods. An army of lackeys sprouts up around them in no time.

All this is naturally a mirage, a short-lived rule. It fades into nothing along with the anarchy, for the liberators finally arrive in the morning.

The first Soviet soldier appears in the block doorway quietly, almost imperceptibly. An officer. A red-faced blond young man. Five armed soldiers are standing behind him. There's a girl among them, too, wavy hair flowing out from underneath her military cap. The submachine guns slung across their chests clatter with their hard steps.

Again, a cacophony of voices crying out; again, misty eyes. The skeletons stretch out their wizened arms; tear-choked cheers erupt.

The officer stops in the middle of the hall. He now looks about, soaking in the scene, the shocking image of Block A, not yet seen by human eyes. Marching right into the muck, he steps closer to the bunks. His whole body shudders.

Hundreds are talking at once. Cried-out grievances flit skyward; pleas flow toward the liberators in Hungarian, German, Yiddish, and Slavic languages.

With stone-cold expressions the Soviet soldiers stare at the haunted house. Their first motions, their first thoughts: *to give* . . . Opening their packs, they scatter what they have upon our beds: bread, sausage, tobacco, rum. The girl soldier adds in a consoling smile.

"Wretched dogs," says the officer, shaking a fist. Revulsion contorts his face.

"Do those who created this hell deserve mercy? No, and no!"

His associates nod. Hatred of the fascist enemy they've been pursuing through three countries flares up. Their fingers tighten against the submachine guns.

The girl passes between the rows of bunks, her cool hand gently caressing the faces and foreheads of the suffering. She is not afraid of the contagion.

The officer addresses us, the interpreter translating his words to German. He announces that within a few hours medical squadrons will arrive along with the troops. We'll get all necessary help without delay.

"Down with fascism! Long live freedom!" With that, he completes his short, soldierly speech.

Two hours later, the medical people really do arrive: a squadron of doctors, nurses, and medics. Farkas guessed right that they immediately ordered a quarantine. That's it for individual initiatives to go home. Later, German women who've been hurriedly rounded up appear and commence with the cleaning and cooking. The mayor of Wüstegiersdorf is ordered to secure a suitable amount of milk, eggs, meat, and flour for the camp each day.

Three days later, those who've already gotten through typhus are transported over to a school building that's been turned into an emergency hospital. German women doctors who are found somewhere or other then wind up staggering about among us, teeth chattering with the horror of guilty consciences, but they don't help us much.

Then I too end up in classroom IV/B—turned hospital room of the Wüstegiersdorf primary school: an unlikely Eden comprising a clean bed, pajamas, edible food, medicine, books, and newspapers. . . .

On a long table in the middle of the room is a smiling bouquet of wildflowers. The springtime sun sprinkles its searinghot gold onto three wide windows. On the cobblestones below us, people, artillery, tanks, motorcycles, cars, and horse-drawn wagons are going up and down day and night. The earth shakes under the weight of trucks topped off with Katyusha rocket launchers.

Soviet artillery, cavalry, infantry, mechanized formations. Polish forces, Czech partisans in yellow blouses, and armed militiamen with red armbands. The carriers of freedom.

We are no longer in Germany: this, too, is happiness. Silesia has become part of Poland. Two days ago Wüstegiersdorf reverted to its former, Polish name. From now on it's called Gierzcze-Pustének.

＊ ＊ ＊

Freedom . . .

Committees and reporters arrive from Prague, Warsaw, Wrocław, and even Budapest. Photojournalists hasten about, delegations take notes for their reports and busy themselves organizing. We hear details of the siege of the Hungarian capital, the heroic fight for Belgrade, Warsaw's biblical agony, the fall of Berlin, a city in ruins.

Like strangers, we take in the view of these people arriving from the outside world, these improbable sons of fortune, these happy beings who'd never put on striped rags. They have first and last names, wedding rings sparkle on their fingers, and they're not ridden with lice. They are the Martians of the universe beyond the barbed wire.

A white-haired Russian nurse, Comrade Tatyana, runs the emergency hospital. She is tender goodness and attentiveness through and through. She speaks Russian, and I reply in Serbian. We somehow understand each other.

I have a fever again. All the excitement of the liberation doesn't fade away without leaving its mark on me. The big events depleted my strength. Time and again, Nurse Tatyana shakes her head when taking my temperature. She stuffs me with pink, yellow, and white puddings and she concocts medicines. The image of the eternal mother shimmers in her patient, old smile. One word reverberates at every turn from the music of her nimble Russian sentences: *svoboda.*

Freedom! With that word, Nurse Tatyana buoys me back to life.

Yes, freedom . . . Freedom everywhere and in everything.

Across the street, freedom glistens on the intricate Gothic letters of the cobwebbed village inn. Freedom smiles upon itself in the red-enameled mirrors of stars on the soldiers' caps. Freedom stirs even in silence; freedom whispers amid all the noise. . . .

Outside, a long and winding village street. Above an endless column of people and cannons, a sweeping, billowing melody stretches out in the radiance of the day: "The Internationale."

They sing.

Afterword

Alexander Bruner, nephew of József Debreczeni
(nom de plume of József Bruner) and Literary
Executor of the Estate of József Debreczeni

Unbeknownst to József at the time, on the day before his own deportation to Auschwitz, his father, Fabian, wrote his last letter—the note to a non-Jewish acquaintance is now housed at the United States Holocaust Memorial Museum—lamenting the dispersal of the family and expressing his hope that "someone be at least somewhat informed about what's the situation here... it is possible that in an hour they will come for me." Fabian; his wife, Sidonia; and József's wife, Lenka, were all murdered, but József fulfilled his father's final wish: when *Cold Crematorium* was first published in 1950, one commentator called it "the harshest, most merciless indictment of Nazism ever written."

József's literary works after the war gave a human voice to history. In a poem called "I Speak With My Father," József asks, "Where is the bloody retribution? Don't the heavens rage?... Who will avenge them?" He was eerily prescient about the diabolical ways in which the Holocaust could be "normalized," rather than recognized as a unique crime in which a modern industrial state attempted—and largely succeeded in Europe—to annihilate an entire people. He knew that for Jews there was the "before" and "after," and nothing would ever be "normal" again.

He instinctively grasped that the perpetrators would try to

hide using a new "uniform" and that, after the world's initial outrage following the war, there would ensue a tendency to negate the
specificity and enormity of the genocide against the Jewish people.
In the ensuing decades, he fought against the ever more insidious
ways in which the memory of the Holocaust was exploited.

My uncle is buried in Belgrade, his tombstone crowned by
a bronze phoenix created by Nandor Glid, a friend and fellow
Holocaust victim, best known for his works in Yad Vashem,
Dachau, and Mauthausen. With the English language edition,
the work is now available to the wider world, and, like the myth-
ological phoenix rising from the ashes, *Cold Crematorium* bears
witness and warns future generations.

I owe deep gratitude to my own father, Mirko Bruner, József's
younger brother, who while stationed as a Yugoslavian diplomat
in Washington, D.C., in the 1950s made numerous attempts to
interest American publishers in translating and publishing the
book in English, only to be rebuffed at every turn; our translator,
Paul Olchváry, for turning the original Hungarian text into vivid
and accessible English; our literary agent, Marc Koralnik, for in-
tuitively grasping the broad international appeal of the work; my
wife, Roberta Presser, for immediately appreciating the enormous
literary quality of *Cold Crematorium*; my friend Steve Ossad for im-
pressing on me the importance of publishing the book for both
personal and historical reasons; my sister Vanda Bruner Colom-
bini and my cousin Vida Šturm for supporting my efforts; and,
of course, Tim Bartlett, Sally Richardson, Michal Shavit, Kevin
Reilly, Charlotte Knight, Dori Weintraub, Mac Nicholas, Kiffin
Steurer, Maya Koffi, and their teams at St. Martin's Press/Macmil-
lan and Jonathan Cape/Vintage/Penguin Random House, for re-
surrecting this "lost" masterpiece.

Translator's Note

The author was from Vojvodina (Hungarian: Vajdaság), a multi-ethnic part of Serbia that has a substantial Hungarian minority and had been part of Austria-Hungary until World War I, and then Yugoslavia. During World War II, Hungary annexed its Bačka (Hungarian: Bácska) region, which reverted in 1945 to the new Yugoslav republic.

Since József Debreczeni and many of the people mentioned in the book were native Hungarian speakers, he used Hungarian place-names in the book's original Hungarian-language text not only for Bačka and Vojvodina but also for other territories beyond the borders of present-day Hungary that were home to many native Hungarians. For ease of reference for readers of the English text, the translation uses the contemporary names of such places (e.g., Novi Sad, for the Serbian city that Hungarian speakers call Újvidék; and Bratislava for the capital of present-day Slovakia, which Hungarians call Pozsony). The glossary section that follows includes the Hungarian names of such places, as well as information on historical figures and terms referred to in the text.

Debreczeni uses some German terms and phrases that, because they were an integral part of the vocabulary of concentration camps, have been preserved in the interest of authenticity, with translations provided. Debreczeni generally provides translations after the first occurrence of the term; the English text uses the same approach. Terms frequently used include:

- *Älteste*—Elder (a general term for "commander")
- *Appell*—Roll call. Assembly of prisoners at which commands were issued, rosters checked, and punishments meted out
- *Blockälteste*—Block Elder
- *Häftling*—Prisoner
- *Kapo*—Prisoner with privileges who oversaw and often brutalized others
- *Lagerälteste*—Camp Elder
- *Lagerschreiber*—Camp Clerk
- *Stubenälteste*—Room Elder (referred to also as "room commander")
- *Wagenälteste*—Wagon Elder

Glossary

Bačka Topola or **Topola** (Hungarian: Bácstapolya or Topolya). A town in the Serbian province of Vojvodina. One of the regional deportation points for Jews sent to Auschwitz/Birkenau.

Baky, László (1898–1946). A leading member of the Hungarian Nazi movement that flourished before and during World War II.

Bratislava (Hungarian: Pozsony). Capital of Slovakia.

Cluj-Napoca (Hungarian: Kolozsvár). Unofficial capital of Romania's Transylvania region.

Dörnhau. See Gross-Rosen.

Endre, László (1895–1946). A Hungarian right-wing politician and collaborator with the Nazis during World War II.

Eule. See Gross-Rosen.

Fürstenstein. See Gross-Rosen.

Gross-Rosen. The village of the same name was the headquarters of a vast network of concentration and slave labor camps in World War II. Debreczeni was imprisoned in the Mülhausen camp in the province of Eule, and in the Fürstenstein and Dörnhau camps. Gross-Rosen is now part of Rogoźnica, in Lower Silesian Voivodeship, Poland.

Hódmezővásárhely. City in southeast Hungary.

Imrédy, Béla (1891–1946). Prime Minister of Hungary from 1938 to 1939, founder of the pro-fascist, anti-Semitic Arrow Cross Party in 1940.

Košice (Hungarian: Kassa). City in Slovakia.

Labor service, or forced labor. A requirement in Hungary of Jewish men and those deemed "politically unreliable" during World

War II after they were prohibited from serving in the regular armed forces.

Lake Balaton. Central Europe's largest lake, located in western Hungary.

Lučenec (Hungarian: Losonc). A town in Slovakia.

Mukachevo (Hungarian: **Munkács**). A city in western Ukraine.

Mülhausen. See Gross-Rosen.

Nagykanizsa. A city in southwestern Hungary near Lake Balaton.

Nové Zámky (Hungarian: Érsekújvár). A town in Slovakia.

Novi Sad (Hungarian: Újvidék). The second largest city in Serbia and the capital of the province of Vojvodina.

Oradea (Hungarian: Nagyvárad). City in Romania's Transylvania region.

Oświęcim. Town in Poland, location of the concentration and death camp of Auschwitz/Birkenau.

Pavelić, Ante (1889–1959). Head of the ultranationalist Ustaše organization and, from 1941 to 1945, dictator of the Independent State of Croatia created in the parts of Yugoslavia occupied by Germany and Italy.

Sombor (Hungarian: Zombor). A city in the province of Vojvodina, Serbia. Debreczeni was arrested in Sombor and moved to Bačka Topola for deportation to Auschwitz/Birkenau.

Subotica (Hungarian: Szabadka). City in the province of Vojvodina, Serbia.

Sztójay, Döme (1883–1946). A Hungarian soldier and diplomat of Serbian origin who served as prime minister of Hungary for a time in 1944.

Topola. See Bačka Topola.

Todt, Fritz (1891–1942). Reich Minister for Armaments and Ammunition who directed the German wartime military economy. Organisation Todt was the military engineering company that supplied industry with forced labor and oversaw the construction of concentration camps.

Uzhhorod (Hungarian: Ungvár). A city in western Ukraine.